Why PRAYER Makes Sense

Why
PRAYER
Makes
Sense

In the Bible, in History, in Your Life Today

Ed Strauss

BARBOUR
PUBLISHING

Published by Barbour Publishing, Inc., P.O. Box 719, Uhrichsville, Ohio 44683, www.barbourbooks.com

Our mission is to publish and distribute inspirational products offering exceptional value and biblical encouragement to the masses.

Printed in the United States of America.

CONTENTS

COMMUNING WITH GOD

BASICS OF PRAYER

FAITH AND PRAYER

PRAYER AND GOD'S WILL

CLAIMING GOD'S PROMISES

FAITH FOR HEALING

WHEN PRAYERS AREN'T ANSWERED

PERSISTING IN PRAYER

BONUS QUESTION

INTRODUCTION

Listen to some people, and you'll hear that prayer is merely wishful thinking or religious oratory. But to those of us who have the Lord Jesus Christ as our Savior, prayer should be much more than simply talking to ourselves or performing a rote task. It can be an amazing time of communication with the Almighty God of the universe.

God is real, and He has the power to do miracles, so genuinely praying accomplishes things and brings about change. From a purely practical viewpoint, therefore, it makes good sense for Christians to pray. This is true whether or not we fully understand how prayer works.

Paul declared that the things of God are "true and reasonable" (Acts 26:25 NIV), and while it's true that some of His doings are mysterious and will only be understood in eternity, many aspects of prayer are simple enough for us to grasp. These seventy-five questions and answers address some of the most frequently asked questions about how and why prayer works and what we can do to pray more effectively. They also explain why some prayers take longer to be answered and why we must often pray so persistently.

But this book delves deeper than mere rational explanations. It was primarily written to encourage you to draw into a more intimate fellowship with your Father in heaven—the source of all hope, peace, wisdom, and miracle-working power. This book also explains how our relationship with Jesus Christ is what gives us authority when we pray and the right to expect that our prayers will be answered.

In these pages you'll meet great Bible characters who, like us, were ordinary men and women until they experienced the power of God through prayer. You'll also read thought-provoking quotes by devoted Christians of past centuries who accomplished great things through prayer—people such as John Wesley (1703–1791), George Whitefield (1714–1770), Adoniram Judson (1788–1850), George Müller (1805–1898), Andrew Murray (1828–1917), Hudson Taylor (1832–1905), C. H. Spurgeon (1834–1892), E. M. Bounds (1835–1913), Mary Slessor (1848–1915), R. A. Torrey (1856–1928), Sundar Singh (1889–1929), and others.

Does prayer actually make a difference? Absolutely! And this book will show you why praying makes sense—in the Bible, in history, and in your life today.

PRAYER AND RELATIONSHIP

1. Is it true that prayer is basically just "talking to God"?

People who make this well-meaning statement are often trying to explain prayer in simple terms for those who have no idea what it is or why they should bother to pray. What they mean is that we must grasp that God is a real Person and that just as we talk with people around us to communicate with them, prayer is us talking to God.

As far as it goes, that's true. Prayer does involve us talking to God. But to say that's all prayer is misses the larger and more important picture of our relationship with our heavenly Father. He is also the holy, all-powerful God, so the communication we have is much deeper than merely "talking" with Him. But neither should it be a stilted, formal relationship.

King Solomon wrote, "God is in heaven and you are on earth" (Ecclesiastes 5:2 NIV), and many people assume that heaven is a great distance away, and prayer is like making a very long-distance phone call. But Jesus said in John 15 that Christians are joined to Him as intimately as a branch is to a grapevine. And Paul tells us that "God has sent forth the Spirit of His Son into your hearts" (Galatians 4:6 NKJV).

Jesus added in John 14:20–23 that He is *in* us and we're *in* Him, and that He and His Father literally dwell inside us. Prayer isn't us praying to a distant God to please notice us and help us. For those who don't know Christ, God *is* distant. But for Christians, prayer is an intimate relationship and continual communication with a holy, loving God dwelling in our hearts.

2. Is prayer mostly me asking God to supply my needs?

Prayer is not simply getting things from God or calling out to God in times of urgent need, though that's the image that readily springs to many people's minds. That's certainly part of it, but prayer is essentially communicating with our heavenly Father, and that communication stems from the relationship that we have with Him.

As Christian missionary to India Sundar Singh said, "Prayer does not mean asking God for all kinds of things we want; it is rather the desire for God Himself, the only Giver of Life. . . . The true spirit of prayer does not consist in asking for blessings, but in receiving Him who is the giver of all blessings, and in living a life of fellowship with Him." How true! Jesus tells us, "Seek first the kingdom of God and His righteousness, and all these things shall be added to you" (Matthew 6:33 NKJV).

Jesus also said that the most important commandment is, "Love the Lord your God with all your heart and with all your soul and with all your mind and with all your strength" (Mark 12:30 NIV). We typically think this refers to loving God during the activities of our daily life, and it does, but how much more when we come to the Father in prayer!

That's why we are to praise and worship God when we begin to pray, before petitioning Him. In fact, our first prayers should be, "Lord, reveal Yourself more fully to me. Help me to love You. Show me Your will. Change me so that I'm more like Jesus in my thoughts and my actions." Then pray for what you need—guidance, protection, finances, healing, and all else.

3. Do we have a right to expect things from God?

A century ago, the famous South African pastor Andrew Murray said, "Think of your place and privilege in Christ, and expect great things!" But what exactly is our place and privilege in Christ that gives us the right to expect things from God, let alone *great* things?

The answer is simple and beautiful: God is our Father and we're His children. The Bible says, "But to all who believed him [Jesus] and accepted him, he gave the right to become children of God" (John 1:12 NLT). As His child, you are heir to His riches. "Because you are his sons, God sent the Spirit of his Son into our hearts, the Spirit who calls out, 'Abba, Father.' So you are. . . God's child; and since you are his child, God has made you also an heir" (Galatians 4:6–7 NIV).

Yes, God is our Father, and it's His good will to care for us. As Jesus tells us, "If you. . . know how to give good gifts to your children, how much more will your Father who is in heaven give good things to those who ask Him!" (Matthew 7:11 NKJV). Max Lucado noted in *He Still Moves Stones* (1993), "You see, it's one thing to accept him as Lord, another to recognize him as Savior—but it's another matter entirely to accept him as Father."

God loved us so much that He sent His Son to die for us (John 3:16), and Paul takes this love to its logical conclusion when he asks: "He that spared not his own Son, but delivered him up for us all, how shall he not with him also freely give us all things?" (Romans 8:32 KJV).

4. Why are we supposed to pray in Jesus' name?

Just before He departed for heaven, Jesus told His disciples, "Most assuredly, I say to you, whatever you ask the Father in My name He will give you. Until now you have asked nothing in My name. Ask, and you will receive" (John 16:23–24 NKJV). So for two thousand years, many Christians have ended their prayers with, "In Jesus' name. Amen."

Most people aren't sure *why* this is required—except that it gives glory to Jesus as God's Son—but Jesus added some powerful promises: "Whatever you ask in My name, that I will do, that the Father may be glorified in the Son. If you ask anything in My name, I will do it" (John 14:13–14 NKJV). And again, "whatever you ask the Father in My name He will give you" (John 16:23 NKJV).

When you make requests in Jesus' name, if you're asking for things *He* wants you to have, it's as though Jesus' name is on an official request form. And the Father won't refuse His Son. As Jesus said, "All that belongs to the Father is mine" (John 16:15 NLT). Everything in heaven—from spiritual riches to the power to supply your physical needs (Philippians 4:19)—belongs to Jesus Christ.

When Ezra went to Judah, he carried a letter from King Artaxerxes in which the king commanded his treasurers to diligently provide whatever Ezra might ask them (Ezra 7:21). Just so, there's power in making requests in Jesus' name, in coming "in the name of the King." And how do you gain such authority and power? As the British preacher C. H. Spurgeon said, "If you want that splendid power in prayer, you must remain in loving, abiding union with the Lord Jesus Christ."

Another thought: saying "Amen" is a very bold and powerful way to end a prayer. *Amen* means, "So let it be!" You're literally praying, "In Jesus' name, so let it be!" This is not a declaration we should make lightly.

5. What gives me authority when I ask for things in prayer?

We're God's children and the Spirit of His Son dwells inside us (Galatians 4:6). But He does more than simply live in our hearts; He desires to be Lord and Master of our lives. We are to submit ourselves to His will. Now, the indwelling Spirit moves *our* spirits to pray, and it's clear that He motivates us to pray according to the will of God (Romans 8:27).

God will answer such prayers because, before we even ask, it is His desire that we have those things or that those changes happen. In the Lord's Prayer we're told to request, "Thy will be done" (Luke 11:2 KJV). And if something is God's *will*, He will provide the *power* to make it happen. But He needs us to ask.

Many Christians past and present have been suddenly prompted to pray for a missionary or a situation, and they obeyed and prayed—sometimes for hours. Later they found out how God had answered. Why did the Holy Spirit *urge*, literally command, them to pray that God would do a miracle if God already willed that it be done? Because He requires us to ask. As C. H. Spurgeon observed, "Whether we like it or not, asking is the rule of the kingdom."

When we're praying for things God tells us to, we can pray in Jesus' name. To do so is to come before God in Jesus' authority, and Jesus said, "All authority in heaven and on earth has been given to me" (Matthew 28:18 NIV). This authority causes the Father to open the treasure houses of heaven, to send forth His power to do the miracle. But let's be clear: we can *only* have such authority if we worship Jesus as Lord, we're submitted to Him, and are praying for His will to be done.

As you may imagine, this cuts selfish, self-centered prayers out of the race, right from the start. But why would we want to pray for something that wasn't God's will?

6. Does God answer the prayers of people who don't know Him?

God knows everything, so He hears every prayer that every person on earth prays. Some people therefore have the idea that He overlooks the fact that people are praying to false gods and idols, that He answers their prayers anyway, and doesn't really mind if their gods get the credit. But God says, "I am the LORD [*Yahweh*], that is My name; and My glory I will not give to another, nor My praise to carved images" (Isaiah 42:8 NKJV).

However, when people cry out to the true God—even though they don't fully know who He is—then yes, He answers. The Greeks worshiped some 370 gods, but Paul pointed out, "As I was. . .considering the objects of your worship, I even found an altar with this inscription: TO THE UNKNOWN GOD. Therefore, *the One whom you worship without knowing*, Him I proclaim to you" (Acts 17:23 NKJV, emphasis added).

Down through history, God has answered the prayers of people who cried out to Him, even though they didn't have a relationship with Him yet. Think of Naaman the Syrian (2 Kings 5:1–17), the Canaanite woman of Phoenicia (Matthew 15:21–28), or the pagan man in Lystra (Acts 14:8–10). They had only a faint idea of who God was, yet they reached out to Him—and He met them.

Consider also Sundar Singh. He was a Sikh and rejected the Gospel. But one night he prayed desperately for seven hours that God would reveal Himself. If not, he determined to throw himself in front of the train at 5:00

a.m. Suddenly a glow filled the room. A man with nail-pierced hands appeared and said, "How long will you deny Me? I died for you. I have given my life for you." And Sundar Singh became a Christian.

There are many similar stories in modern times, especially in the Muslim world. And as many of us also can testify, even before we were Christians, God heard our cries and answered our prayers to bring us to Him.

7. Isn't it the power of "the Universe" that answers prayers?

The book *The Secret* by Rhonda Byrne popularized the idea that it's not a personal God who answers prayers, but rather an abstract force (which she calls "the Universe"), a law as sure as the law of gravity, that's giving people what they desire. Since it's supposedly not the God of the Bible at work, answers to prayer are available to people of all religions—even no religion—so long as they can muster up enough concentrated, positive thoughts.

Because Byrne quotes Matthew 21:22 and

Mark 11:24 (on page 54), many Christians assume that the principles she teaches are scriptural. They don't realize that the many people she quotes in her book are prominent New Age teachers. In direct contradiction to them, just before stating the prayer principle in Mark 11:24, Jesus stated, "Have faith in God" (vs. 22)—the God of the Bible.

One of the foundational principles *The Secret* (2006) teaches is "the law of attraction," that if you want something all you have to do is intently desire it, constantly visualize and generate feelings that it's yours now—and you'll have it. You supposedly attract what you think about.

Byrne warns, however, that the Universe cannot discriminate between what you *want* or *don't* want. Thinking about something will bring it on you. As she says on page 15, if you think, "I don't want to catch the flu," you're telling the Universe, "I want the flu." Following this line of reasoning, David's prayers in the Psalms to be delivered from his enemies would've had the opposite effect and brought calamity upon him. And Jesus' instructions to pray "deliver us from evil" (Matthew 6:13 KJV) would've been catastrophically bad advice.

We know that's not the case. Byrne is mistaken. The God of the Bible, the Father of Jesus Christ—not some impersonal force—is the One who answers prayer.

8. Why do I need to pray if God already knows everything I need?

God is *omniscient*, which means all-knowing. He knows everything. He knows the number of hairs on your head and even knows what every single sparrow on earth is doing at any given moment (Luke 12:6–7). Such omniscience may be incomprehensible to us, but that's precisely the point: God is God and is too vast for our minds to comprehend. The question this raises, however, is, "Why bother to pray if God already knows absolutely everything that I need?"

Jesus said, "And when you pray, do not keep on babbling like pagans, for they think they will be heard because of their many words. Do not be like them, for your Father knows what you need before you ask him" (Matthew 6:7–8 NIV). The pagans thought that the longer they prayed, the more likely it was that their gods would *finally* hear them. They also had to make sure that their uninformed gods knew what they needed. When we state our requests simply, we acknowledge that God already knows our need.

Furthermore, God isn't a distant, uncaring deity. He's our loving Father. We're His children. We have a relationship with Him. That's why He wants us to speak to Him with trust. Prayer is, after all, not some attempt to impress heaven with our eloquence, but sincere communication with a loving Father. So we must talk to Him from our hearts.

Another reason to pray is that even though *God* knows what we require, He wants *us* to fully realize our needs and to be aware that He alone can help us. Prayer is acknowledging our inability and limitations and God's ability and unlimited power. When we do this, we admit our dependence on Him. We're also verbalizing that He is God, and this is a form of worship. So talk to God today. He says, "Call to Me, and I will answer you" (Jeremiah 33:3 NKJV).

9. Does God need or require us to ask before He does anything?

Since God knows what we need before we ask Him (Matthew 6:8), some people wonder why He requires us to ask Him at all. Why doesn't He just go ahead and do it—especially if it's His will anyway? Isn't God all-powerful? Isn't He sovereign? Doesn't whatever happens happen because He wills it happen?

Yes, God is all-powerful. And He definitely wills that certain, specific things happen regarding individuals and nations. Yet, what He wills doesn't automatically happen. For example, Jesus said that "it is not the will of your Father who is in heaven that one of these little ones should perish" (Matthew 18:14 NKJV). Yet, unfortunately, many *do* perish.

Although God can do anything, He has chosen to partner with weak, fallible humanity. He desires to work in and through us. We're not only His hands and feet to show the world His love in practical ways—but our Father has also, in large measure, limited Himself to acting in response to our concerned prayers. Yes, even for things that are explicitly His will.

A clear example of this is how, centuries before He freed the Hebrews from slavery in Egypt, God stated that this was His will (Genesis 15:13–16). Yet He only began to take action after they cried out desperately and repeatedly (Exodus 2:23–25; 3:7–9).

Another example is when, after a three-year drought had parched the land of Israel, God told Elijah, "Go and present yourself to Ahab, and I will send rain on the land" (1 Kings 18:1 NIV). It was God's will to send rain. Elijah obeyed, but God still didn't send rain until Elijah prayed fervently and repeatedly for Him to do so (1 Kings 18:41–45; see also James 5:17–18).

Again, God stated that after His people had been captives in Babylon for seventy years, He would free them to return to their land (Jeremiah 29:10). Yet God only acted after Daniel prayed desperately for Him to fulfill His word (Daniel 9:1–19; Ezra 1:1–3).

10. Do you mean that God won't do anything unless we pray for Him to?

Yes and no. God established natural laws and created the world according to His will, for the benefit of humanity. "He makes His sun rise on the evil and on the good, and sends rain on the just and on the unjust" (Matthew 5:45 NKJV), and gives us "rain from heaven and crops in their seasons" (Acts 14:17 NIV). God simply went ahead and performed His will in these things without anyone requesting Him to.

He also set spiritual laws in place. "God is not mocked; for whatever a man sows, that he will also reap" (Galatians 6:7 NKJV). He has repeatedly promised to bless obedience and judge disobedience—in this life and in the next. God has clearly declared His intentions in these matters.

But having created the world and set up both spiritual and physical laws by which it runs, God then made humanity in His own image and ordained us to rule the earth and have dominion over it (Genesis 1:26–28). So the Bible tells us, "The heaven, even the heavens, are the LORD's; but the earth He has given to the children of men" (Psalm 115:16 NKJV). Yet we're told, "*He* does according to *His* will. . . among the inhabitants of the earth" (Daniel 4:35 NKJV, emphasis added). So *whose* will is done on earth? Jesus instructed us to pray, "Thy will be done in earth, as it is in heaven" (Matthew 6:10 KJV). God intends for *His* will to be done *through* us. We have access to His power to bring about His will—if we pray.

David Brainerd, missionary to the Native Americans, said, "The idea that everything would happen exactly as it does regardless of whether we pray or not is a specter that haunts the minds of many who sincerely profess belief in God. It makes prayer psychologically impossible." But we *must* pray. E. M. Bounds explained, "God's cause is committed to men; God commits Himself to men. Praying men are the vice-regents of God; they do His work and carry out His plans."

COMMUNING WITH GOD

11. Is worshiping God an essential part of prayer?

Many people, when they pray, simply state what they need and sign off with, "In Jesus' name, amen." Not only are they unaware that they're carelessly invoking all the power of Jesus' name, but they've also often spent little time in the presence of the Lord, acknowledging that He's the all-powerful God who is *able* to answer prayer. Yet the Bible commands us to take time to quiet our hearts before Him: "Be still, and know that I am God" (Psalm 46:10 KJV). It also commands us to praise and worship Him: "Give unto the LORD the glory due unto his name; worship the LORD in the beauty of holiness" (Psalm 29:2 KJV).

As Andrew Murray said, "Each time, before you intercede, be quiet first, and worship God in His glory. Think of what He can do, and how He delights to hear the prayers of His redeemed people. Think of your place and privilege in Christ, and expect great things!"

The principles Murray mentions dramatically increase the likelihood of your prayers being answered so are well worth a closer look. He says to (1) be quiet first, and (2) worship God. Then think of (3) what He can do, and (4) how He delights to hear your prayers. Meditate on (5) your place and rights in Christ, and (6) you'll be encouraged to expect great things. Then you're ready to begin petitioning.

Of course, when you're in the middle of a hectic day or facing a sudden emergency, you need to blurt out your requests. What we're talking about here is when you're dedicating a chunk of time to meet with God—your morning prayers before the day begins, your evening prayers, and other special times of prayer.

12. What does it mean to "enter into God's presence"?

The Psalms command, "Let us come before his presence with thanksgiving" and "come before his presence with singing" (Psalm 95:2; 100:2 KJV). In Old Testament times, the temple in Jerusalem was the main place God manifested Himself. He was sometimes literally present in the innermost chamber called the Holy of Holies. Thus, when people entered the temple, they went with an attitude of reverence and awe, offering thanks to God for His goodness and singing songs of praise.

Likewise today, when we worship God, it brings us into His presence. As Christians we must remember that we're not praying to a distant deity who may or may not be listening, but are entering into the very throne room of God. "Let us therefore come boldly unto the throne of grace, that we may obtain mercy, and find grace to help in time of need" (Hebrews 4:16 KJV). You have an audience with your Father, and He's attentive to what you're saying.

But have you ever prayed and, *while* you were praying, realized that although you were speaking words, you didn't really have faith that you were actually talking to God? You weren't quite sure that He was listening? The problem may be that you failed to enter His presence *before* you began praying.

The evangelist R. A. Torrey described the solution, saying that "the first thing we should do is to see to it that we really get an audience with God, that we really get into His very presence. Before a word of petition is offered, we should have the definite consciousness that we are talking to God, and should believe that He is listening and is going to grant the thing that we ask of Him."

Before you begin asking God for things, make sure that you've entered into His presence. And one of the best ways to do that is with thanksgiving and praise.

13. Why is it important to have daily prayer time?

If you're new to prayer or aren't in the habit of praying regularly, you might have rolled your eyes when reading about "morning prayers and evening prayers." You're probably a busy father, mother, or student who already has to get up early to do each day's work, and your evenings are either taken up with housework or are when you hope to relax. You may wonder where you're supposed to get the time to pray more, and feel you're doing well enough to pray when problems hit.

But you can't develop a deep relationship with the Father by just praying on the run or only when you need Him. God is the source of the power you need to solve your many problems big and small, so it makes sense to spend *time* in His presence, plugged into Him.

Throughout history, God's people understood that the most effective way to start their days was with prayer. David wrote, "Listen to my voice in the morning, Lord. Each morning I bring my requests to you and wait expectantly" (Psalm 5:3 NLT). And Jesus, God's Son, often talked to the Father then. "Very early in the morning. . .he prayed" (Mark 1:35 NIV).

In fact, the Jews typically set aside time three times every day—morning, noon, and evening—to pray (see Psalm 55:17; Daniel 6:10). Generally you'll find mornings and evenings most conducive to spending meaningful chunks of time with God, but it also helps to pause for even a few minutes during the day to commit your decisions and your actions to Him and to seek His guidance.

14. What if I find prayer boring? Should I do it anyway?

The short answer is yes. The problem many people have is that even if they *can* carve out fifteen minutes—or even an hour—to pray every day, they find it difficult to apply themselves. They find prayer boring. Praying can be hard work. Or they don't know what to pray about, so their minds constantly drift.

When you have a desperate need and you're almost at your wit's end, however, you know *exactly* what to pray about. You're not thinking how boring it is. Yet much of the time, our problems, though pressing, don't seem unmanageable. . .yet. And as long as we seem to have things under control, we don't feel a need to ask for God's help.

An early missionary to Nigeria, Mary

Slessor, candidly admitted, "Praying is harder work than doing, at least I find it so." Disciplining yourself to pray is like starting an exercise regimen: you know you need to get in shape, you need to put the time in—but it seems so boring and you begin to question whether the payoff is really worth it. Or establishing a healthier diet: it can be hard to follow through with, and you start to question whether healthy living is all that it's made out to be. But as with exercise and healthy eating, if you follow through on prayer faithfully, it has many long-term benefits.

Besides, experience has taught us that it's not wise to put something off until the situation gets desperate. We must understand that we need God. When we feel insufficient to go through a day without His power, with that sense of need comes more of a willingness and desire to pray. Then, although it may still be difficult at times, we'll have the will to persevere.

15. Why do some Christians spend an hour or more in prayer every day?

When you hear about Christians who spend an hour or two praying every day, you might think, "These people must have some serious *time* on their hands! Either that or they're a pastor or a missionary whose job description includes praying that much. But I'm too busy to pray more than ten minutes a day—fifteen minutes at the very most." Some busy mothers of very busy children seize much of their prayer time while doing dishes and other tasks.

If you can't spare an hour, then you can't. Give what you can. But for two thousand years, many Christians have been moved by Jesus' question. He had asked His disciples to pray with Him, but they fell asleep. So Jesus asked, "Could you not watch with Me one hour?" (Matthew 26:40 NKJV). The implication was that praying for an hour wasn't too much to ask.

Our problem, however, is that we're often in such a hurry to rush into the day that we skimp on prayer and head out. . .mostly in our own power. Spiritual giants of the past such as

Martin Luther, John Wesley, George Müller, and others spent two or more hours in prayer daily and attributed their success to this. And while there's no hard-and-fast rule as to how much time we "ought" to pray, the American pastor E. M. Bounds advised, "In general it is best to have at least one hour alone with God before engaging in anything else."

If you're simply not a morning person, but are more awake in the evening and have more time available then, you might want to do *most* of your praying the evening before. But by all means, spend some time in the morning acknowledging your Father and asking for His wisdom and power.

16. How can I "pray without ceasing" as the Bible says?

Paul wrote, "Pray without ceasing" (1 Thessalonians 5:17 KJV). In the New International Version this short verse is even shorter, reading, "pray continually." What precisely does this mean? Many Christians wonder if they're literally supposed to pray nonstop all day. It doesn't sound like safe advice for someone operating heavy machinery, and doesn't even seem feasible for a teacher delivering a lecture. How can you possibly split your attention between prayer and work when your job often requires most of your attention?

One famous man of faith, George Müller, was once asked how much time he spent in prayer. He answered, "Hours every day." Then he added, "But I live in the spirit of prayer. I pray as I walk and when I lie down and when I arise. And the answers are always coming." If you live in a continual attitude of prayer, your heart and mind will be in tune with God, even when your duties don't permit you to say a focused prayer.

If you obey the most important commandment—"Love the Lord your God with all your heart and with all your soul and with all your mind and with all your strength" (Mark 12:30 NIV)—you'll naturally look to God all day long. You'll be thanking Him for victories and blessings, great and small, and you'll automatically commit your problems and concerns to Him as they come up.

It may take sustained effort to get in the habit at first, but after a while you'll find yourself praying and communing with your Father throughout the day.

17. Is prayer a two-way conversation? Will God actually speak to me?

Yes, God speaks to *all* Christians. After all, the Bible is His Word and when we read it we're hearing God speak. But only the Lord can truly open our eyes to its truth. That's why it's important to pray, as the psalmist did, "Open my eyes that I may see wonderful things in your law" (Psalm 119:18 NIV). When we read, God can do as he did to the travelers to Emmaus: "Then he opened their minds to understand the Scriptures" (Luke 24:45 NLT).

When we earnestly pray for direction, God often speaks to us by bringing a verse from the scriptures to our minds. Jesus promised, "But the Helper, the Holy Spirit. . .will teach you all things, and bring to your remembrance all things that I said to you" (John 14:26 NKJV). God's Spirit still teaches us today, and He often does this by reminding us of specific words of Jesus.

In addition, many Christians have experienced God guiding them, not with literal words per se, but by His Spirit impressing on their heart that they *should* or should *not* do something. "When the Spirit of truth comes, he will guide you into all truth" (John 16:13 NLT).

Still other Christians testify that God has spoken to them in "a still small voice" (1 Kings 19:12 KJV). They don't normally claim that these are audible words, simply that a message has impressed itself upon their mind. This is wonderful when it happens.

We do well to exercise caution, however, since we sometimes hear from our own active imaginations and assume we're hearing God (see Jeremiah 23:21). In fact, *whatever* way we believe that God is speaking, we're wise to make sure that it lines up with scripture. But God *does* speak—and often His answer is the miracle of an answered prayer.

18. How will prayer affect me?

Often, our purpose in prayer is to worship God and to petition Him to meet our needs, but one of prayer's primary benefits is that it transforms our own lives. It makes us more godly. This is because prayer isn't just us trying to convince God to give us things we want, but praying for His will to be done in our lives (see Matthew 6:10; 26:39).

Paul says that Christians "have the mind of Christ" (1 Corinthians 2:16 NKJV). But if we're honest, we realize that we have this gift in limited measure. How do we receive more of it? E. M. Bounds explained, "Prayer makes a godly man, and puts within him the mind of Christ, the mind of humility, of self-surrender, of service, of pity, and of prayer. If we really pray, we will become more like God." He added that "personal Christian graces have their being, bloom, and fruitage in prayer."

As Christians, we should desire to become more like Jesus. It is, in fact, the Father's will that we "be conformed to the image of his Son" (Romans 8:29 KJV). Time spent in prayer, communing with God, is the main catalyst for this change. "And we all, who. . .contemplate the Lord's glory, are being transformed into his image with ever-increasing glory, which comes from the Lord" (2 Corinthians 3:18 NIV).

Of course, an important part of the transforming process is to obey God's will. If we're to truly have the mind of Christ, then we must be willing to say, like Jesus, "I do not seek My own will but the will of the Father who sent Me" (John 5:30 NKJV). The apostle John's letter commented: "Those who say they live in God should live their lives as Jesus did" (1 John 2:6 NLT). God gives His Holy Spirit to those who *obey* Him (Acts 5:32), and the more of the Spirit of God we have in our hearts, the more we'll be like Him.

BASICS OF PRAYER

19. Did Jesus mean for us to pray the Lord's Prayer repeatedly?

When one of Jesus' disciples asked, "Lord, teach us to pray," Jesus replied, "When you pray, say: Our Father in heaven, hallowed be Your name. Your kingdom come. Your will be done on earth as it is in heaven. Give us day by day our daily bread. And forgive us our sins, for we also forgive everyone who is indebted to us. And do not lead us into temptation, but deliver us from the evil one" (Luke 11:1–4 NKJV).

The Lord's Prayer, as it's called, is a model of simplicity and covers all the bases: a Christian praying this gives praise to God, prays for His will to be done, and prays for his or her most pressing human needs. Many people therefore memorize this prayer and recite it word for word, often several times a day. . .sometimes several times in a row. But while praying this prayer can be an enriching experience, it's a model, not some magical mantra.

This is demonstrated by the fact that there isn't just one official version of this prayer. The wording in Luke 11:1–4 is slightly different from the more frequently quoted version of Matthew 6:9–13. This is because Jesus taught this prayer on different occasions, and because the prayer's essence and spirit is the main point, not the literal words.

Also, note that when Jesus' disciples asked, "Lord, teach us to pray," He first taught them the Lord's Prayer (vs. 1–4); then He taught them the importance of persistent prayer (vs. 5–8); then He taught that God answers sincere prayers (vs. 9–10); He reinforced this by teaching that God answers because He isn't capricious, but good (vs. 11–13). In answer to the disciples' request, Jesus taught much more than a ritual prayer.

20. Why do Christians pray repetitive prayers when Jesus said not to?

Jesus said, "And when you pray, do not use vain repetitions as the heathen do. For they think that they will be heard for their many words" (Matthew 6:7 NKJV). Yet only a short while later He advised, "Keep on asking and it will be given to you." This verse is usually translated, "Ask, and it will be given to you" (Matthew 7:7 NKJV), but the original Greek verb tense for *ask* literally means "keep on asking."

And that's precisely what people in the Bible did. Elijah prayed for rain seven times (1 Kings 18:42–44). And when Jesus was praying in the Garden of Gethsemane, He prayed three times "saying the same words" (Matthew 26:44 NKJV).

There's no contradiction, however. Their prayers were repeated but they weren't "vain [empty, useless] repetitions." They were desperate, heartfelt cries to God. So yes, there are times when we *need* to pray repeatedly for the same thing. E. M. Bounds declared, "We are to press the matter, not with vain repetitions, but with urgent repetitions. We repeat, not to count the times, but to gain the prayer. We cannot quit praying because heart and soul are in it."

And it's biblical to pray persistently for the same thing. The Bible says: "You who call on the Lord, give yourselves no rest, and give him no rest till he establishes Jerusalem and makes her the praise of the earth" (Isaiah 62:6–7 NIV). (See also Luke 18:1–8.)

As the renowned evangelist D. L. Moody wrote in *Prevailing Prayer: What Hinders It?* (1884), "Some people think God does not like to be troubled with our constant coming and asking. The only way to trouble God is not to come at all."

21. Do I have to pray out loud? Should I kneel and close my eyes?

It's customary to pray out loud, and there are commonsense reasons for it. For one thing, actually speaking the words—not merely thinking them—helps us stay focused and keeps our minds from wandering. For the same reason, most people find it helpful to close their eyes when they pray: they can better focus on God and not be distracted by things around them.

David prayed, "Hear my prayer, O God; give ear to the words of my mouth" (Psalm 54:2 KJV), and some people insist that you must pray out loud for your prayers to be effective. But David also said, "Before a word is on my tongue you, LORD, know it completely" (Psalm 139:4 NIV), and he implored, "Give ear to my words, O LORD, consider my meditation" (Psalm 5:1 KJV). In addition, when Hannah prayed, she was so troubled that she couldn't even speak, yet God wonderfully answered her prayer (1 Samuel 1:10–17, 26–27).

As to whether you should kneel, yes, it's customary to do so. When King Solomon dedicated the temple of God, he knelt down and prayed (2 Chronicles 6:13). And when God's glory filled the temple, the Israelites "bowed their faces to the ground on the pavement, and worshiped" (2 Chronicles 7:3 NKJV). Jesus knelt when He prayed and so did Paul (Luke 22:41; Acts 20:36).

Kneeling before the Father is a form of worship, and reminds us that He is the all-powerful God whom we're presenting our petitions to. Nevertheless, kneeling is not mandatory, and many times in the Bible people stood when they worshiped or prayed (Exodus 33:10; Luke 18:13).

22. What did Jesus mean when He said, "Go into your closet and pray"?

Jesus had just warned His disciples about Pharisees who stood in public places where many people passed, and prayed—supposedly to God. In reality, they were putting on a show for others, hoping to be admired for praying so much. Jesus said that such people had all the reward they were going to get. God wouldn't answer such feigned prayers.

Jesus then said, "But thou, when thou prayest, enter into thy closet, and when thou hast shut thy door, pray to thy Father which is in secret; and thy Father which seeth in secret shall reward thee openly" (Matthew 6:6 KJV). A number of people, misunderstanding this verse, literally enter their clothes closets to pray. However, the Greek word translated "closet" is *tameion*, and means "inner chamber." The idea is to enter into a private chamber such as a bedroom and shut the door so that only God sees and hears you praying. Most modern translations reflect this understanding.

Because of the wording of the King James translation, some Christians, when they talk about personal prayer, refer to it as "time spent in the closet" or "shutting themselves in with God." It is also called "the secret place," because we are told to pray in secret. This imagery is repeated in Psalm 91:1 (KJV) which reads, "He that dwelleth in the secret place of the most High shall abide under the shadow of the Almighty."

Some people draw the conclusion that Jesus was saying that Christians are never to pray in public, but only in private. However, there are plenty of examples in the Bible of God's people praying in public meetings—especially during times of dire need—and God hears and answers such prayers if they're sincere and not done to impress others.

23. How does it help to get others to pray for me as well?

When we pray for something, we personally need to have faith that God will answer. When two blind men asked Jesus to heal them, He asked, "Do you believe that I am able to do this?" When they replied, "Yes, Lord." Jesus said, "According to your faith let it be done to you" (Matthew 9:28–29 NIV). God expects us to have faith, since "without faith it is impossible to please him" (Hebrews 11:6 KJV). With a few rare exceptions, we cannot depend on others to have faith *for* us or to pray to God *for* us.

However, it's a perfectly sound prayer principle to request other Christians to pray *with* us—whether for finances, for healing, for protection, for a wayward loved one, or whatever. Jesus said, "If two of you agree here on earth concerning anything you ask, my Father in heaven will do it for you" (Matthew 18:19 NLT).

When the apostle Paul was about to head into a dangerous situation, he asked the Christians in Rome to pray with him: "Now I beg you, brethren, through the Lord Jesus Christ. . .that you strive together with me in prayers to God for me" (Romans 15:30 NKJV).

Paul definitely believed in praying for others. He was constantly praying for individuals and entire churches (see Romans 1:9–10; Ephesians 1:16; 2 Timothy 1:3). So next time someone in your church or your Bible study group asks, "Are there any prayer requests?" don't be shy. Ask others to pray for and with you.

24. Why do Christians believe that prayer meetings have power?

Throughout the Old Testament, during times of national emergencies, God's people gathered to pray (2 Chronicles 20:1–13). And there are several examples of the early Christians assembling for prayer meetings. The church was launched on its mission after all the disciples prayed for ten days together. As a result, they were filled with the Holy Spirit and three thousand people were saved (Acts 1:13–14; 2:1–4; 40–41).

When they were suffering persecution, "they raised their voices to God with one accord." And the result? "When they had prayed, the place where they were assembled together was shaken; and they were all filled with the Holy Spirit, and they spoke the word of God with boldness" (Acts 4:24, 31 NKJV).

Later, when Peter was arrested and in prison, "constant prayer was offered to God for him by the church" and "many were gathered together praying" at the house of Mary, the mother of John (Acts 12:5, 12 NKJV). God answered their prayers and sent an angel to set Peter free.

Many churches, therefore, hold prayer meetings before each Sunday service and during the week as well. The powerful British preacher C. H. Spurgeon observed: "The condition of the church may be very accurately gauged by its prayer meetings. . .from it we may judge of the amount of divine working among a people. If God be near a church, it must pray."

A prayer meeting can consist of as few as two or three individuals and still have a powerful effect. Jesus said, "For where two or three are gathered together in my name, there am I in the midst of them" (Matthew 18:20 KJV).

25. What is "intercessory prayer"?

You'll sometimes hear people talking about "intercessors," or "making intercession in prayer," or "interceding for someone." What do these expressions mean? Well, by definition *intercession* is "entreaty in favor of another, especially a prayer or petition to God in behalf of another." It also means "mediation in a dispute."

The dispute between God and humanity was our sin, but when Jesus died on the cross, He successfully mediated and reconciled us to God. Jesus *still* pleads our case to the Father since "He always lives to make intercession for [us]" (Hebrews 7:25 NKJV). As Paul wrote, "It is Christ who died, and furthermore is also risen, who is even at the right hand of God, who also makes intercession for us" (Romans 8:34 NKJV).

We're also called to intercede for others. "I urge. . .that petitions, prayers, intercession and thanksgiving be made for all people" (1 Timothy 2:1 NIV). As the pastor Dutch Sheets explains in his book, *Intercessory Prayer* (1996), "Intercessory prayer is an extension of the ministry of Jesus through His Body, the Church, whereby we mediate between God and humanity for the purpose of reconciling the world to Him, or between Satan and humanity for the purpose of enforcing the victory of Calvary."

Men and women who frequently pray for others or for needs in the church are called prayer warriors or intercessors—but we should *all* be intercessors, asking God to have mercy on others, to protect them, to reveal the truth to them, and to save them. As John Calvin stressed, "To make intercession for men is the most powerful and practical way in which we can express our love for them."

FAITH AND PRAYER

26. Why did Jesus repeatedly say we must have faith when we pray?

Jesus said, "You can pray for anything, and if you have faith, you will receive it" (Matthew 21:22 NLT). "Everything is possible for one who believes" (Mark 9:23 NIV). "Truly I tell you, if anyone. . .does not doubt in their heart but believes that what they say will happen, it will be done for them. Therefore I tell you, whatever you ask for in prayer, believe that you have received it, and it will be yours" (Mark 11:22–24 NIV).

You notice that Jesus assumed that His fellow Jews would pray—and they *did*, often. But much of their praying had become sterile rituals, done more from a sense of religious duty than out of a belief that God would actually hear and answer. Many people's prayers today lack faith as well. This is especially true for those who don't have a relationship with God, but even some Christians exhibit surprisingly little faith when they pray.

R. A. Torrey wrote in *How to Pray* (1900), "If we are to pray with power we must pray with faith." Prayers without faith simply can't please God, because "without faith it is impossible to please Him, for he who comes to God must believe that He is, and that He is a rewarder of those who diligently seek Him" (Hebrews 11:6 NKJV). This verse gives two reasons why we must believe when we pray:

First, we must believe that God (the all-powerful God who created the world) exists and that He actually has the *power* to answer prayer. Second, we must have faith that God loves to reward our sincere prayers. It's not enough to know that God has the power to do so. We must believe that He's also *willing* to answer our prayers. And it's much easier to believe that God is willing to answer our prayers if we know that we desire *His* will, not our own.

27. What exactly is faith?

"Now faith is the substance of things hoped for, the evidence of things not seen" (Hebrews 11:1 NKJV). The Greek word translated as "substance" is *hupostasis*, and in the NIV Interlinear Greek-English New Testament its meaning is given as "reality." Thus, "faith is the *reality* of things hoped for." Faith is not the actual "things hoped for," but it's the reality of those things. But what exactly does *that* mean?

The Amplified Bible gives further insight: "Now faith is the assurance (the confirmation, the title deed) of the things [we] hope for, being the proof of things [we] do not see and the conviction of their reality [faith perceiving as real fact what is not revealed to the senses]" (Hebrews 11:1 AMP).

A title deed is an authoritative document. While it's only a piece of paper and not the actual house or property it speaks of, if your name is on a title deed and it's notarized by the proper authorities, it's proof that you own tangible real estate. If you haven't seen the properties yet—say you received them as an inheritance—they aren't "revealed to the senses" but you have a "conviction of their reality." Why? Because you have the title deed.

When you realize what a solid reality faith is, you might wonder why it doesn't seem to work for some people. They believe for a while then give up without receiving what they were praying for. Why is this? Often it's because they have, at some point, discarded their title deed. "So do not throw away this confident trust in the Lord. Remember the great reward it brings you!" (Hebrews 10:35 NLT).

28. Why do some people have great faith and others have no faith?

Everyone has faith—even atheists. "God has dealt to each one a measure of faith" (Romans 12:3 NKJV). For example, you may have a high level of faith in the postal system. You trust that when you a drop a letter in the mailbox that it will—perhaps 95 percent of the time—reach its destination. Or you may have a great deal of confidence in your abilities to do a certain job or to solve complex problems. Or you may trust in money.

The issue, however, is that not everyone has a lot of faith in the unseen God. That's why Jesus urged people, "Have faith in *God*" (Mark 11:22 KJV, emphasis added). This is why Paul wrote, "Teach those who are rich in this world not to be proud and not to trust in their money, which is so unreliable. Their trust should be in God" (1 Timothy 6:17 NLT).

As you read the Gospels, you find that again and again Jesus was dismayed by how little faith certain people had—including His own disciples. On the other hand, Jesus praised the great faith that a Roman centurion had. "When Jesus heard this, he. . .said, 'I tell you, I have not found such great faith even in Israel' " (Luke 7:9 NIV). (Read the entire story in Luke 7:1–10.)

The centurion's great faith was based on his own down-to-earth, practical experience: he knew that when he gave an order it would be obeyed, implicitly and immediately. So when he heard of the authority Jesus had over sickness, he correctly transferred his under-standing of military workings to Jesus, reason-ing that He had but to speak the word and what He said would be done.

29. What can I do to get faith or to help the faith I have grow?

If you realize that your faith isn't strong, and you don't have the confidence that your prayers will be answered but only have a nebulous hope that God might *possibly* give you what you pray for, there are steps you can take to increase your faith.

First, you must earnestly desire greater faith and, like the disciples, plead, "Increase [my] faith." Or cry out, "Lord, I believe; help my unbelief!" (Luke 17:5; Mark 9:24 NKJV). God will certainly answer such sincere requests, though it may take time. As C. H. Spurgeon said, "There has never been an instance yet of a man really seeking spiritual blessings from God without his receiving them." When God increases your faith and you see your prayers being answered in a miraculous manner, then do all you can to encourage this gift.

Paul wrote to Timothy, "I remind you to stir up the gift of God which is in you through the laying on of my hands" (2 Timothy 1:6 NKJV). Or as the New International Version puts it, "I remind you to fan into flame the gift of God, which is in you." Paul had prayed for God to give Timothy a spiritual gift, and now that this gift was in Timothy's possession, he needed to stir it up, to fan the burning ember into a fire.

You do this by acting on faith when it comes to you, however small it seems in the beginning. Obey God and use it. Put it into practice. If you have faith for small day-to-day miracles, then constantly pray for such miracles. By so doing you fan the flames of your faith to believe God for the larger miracles you need as well. And remember, you'll have more faith God will answer if you're certain that you're praying for things within His will.

30. Do reading and meditating on God's Word increase faith?

Yes! They definitely do. One of the best ways to fan the flame of your faith is by spending time in prayer and devotions, and by reading God's Word. "So then faith cometh by hearing, and hearing by the word of God" (Romans 10:17 KJV). In the first century AD, few people could read, so they depended upon literate Christians to read the Word of God aloud. These days, most people are literate—so faith comes directly from reading the Word of God.

Just as we eat physical food in order to grow and have strength, so we must read God's Word to grow in spiritual strength. Our faith increases when we study and meditate on the Scriptures, especially the teachings of Christ in the New Testament.

If you're experiencing doubt in certain areas, don't put up with it! Study God's Word, seek out answers, and pray for the Lord to increase your faith. God intended that the miracles and wisdom and the truth of the scriptures would inspire your faith. John stated that the reason these things were written was "that you may believe" (John 20:31 NIV).

However, you must read with an open heart and receptive mind. Just reading the Bible doesn't, in itself, automatically increase faith. In Jesus' day, many scribes who daily copied out the scriptures didn't have much faith in them (Matthew 23:23). In other cases, "the word which they heard did not profit them, not being mixed with faith in those who heard it" (Hebrews 4:2 NKJV). But if you sincerely pray for God to increase your faith, and read your Bible with an open heart, your faith will grow.

31. Do we choose to have faith? If we lack faith, is this often a choice?

We consciously or unconsciously make decisions whether we're *willing* to have faith in God or not. Jesus was often disappointed that His disciples lacked faith. When they were fearful during a storm, He asked, "Why are you so afraid? Do you still have no faith?" (Mark 4:40 NIV) He asked again, "Where is your faith?" (Luke 8:25 NIV). On another occasion "He rebuked their unbelief and hardness of heart, because they did not believe those who had seen Him after He had risen" (Mark 16:14 NKJV). As you see, He *expected* them to believe more.

Matthew and Mark both describe Jesus visiting His hometown, Nazareth. Please pause to read Matthew 13:53–58 and Mark 6:1–6. Notice that Mark 6:2 (NIV) says that the people of Nazareth were "amazed" that Jesus exhibited such wisdom and miraculous powers. For His part, Jesus was "amazed at their lack of faith" (verse 6).

Their faith was so unreasonably, stubbornly small because they were *refusing* to believe. Why? Because the people of Nazareth "knew" that Jesus was nothing more than a local boy, a common manual laborer. They thought they knew all about Him, so the fact that He now had miraculous powers confused and bothered them rather than convinced them.

Can we actually choose to have faith—or to not have it? Yes, people do this all the time. Jesus talked about those who "when they hear, receive the word with joy; and these have no root, which *for a while believe*, and in time of temptation fall away" (Luke 8:13 KJV, emphasis added). Did what tempted them convince them that their faith was wrong? No. But after they gave in to temptation, they *chose* to discard their faith and stop believing.

The good news, however, is that you can make a conscious decision to be willing to believe, and God will honor that.

32. How can I tell how much faith I have?

The Bible describes several categories of faith, ranging from stubborn disbelief to great faith.

The first group is people with an agenda of unbelief. They don't believe and don't *want* to believe. In Jesus' day, many Jews "hardened their hearts" (John 12:40 NKJV) and determined not to be convinced. They weren't open to being persuaded, so "although He had done so many signs before them, they did not believe in Him" (John 12:37 NKJV).

The second group is people who don't believe because they just can't see the sense in it. They're skeptical. The people of Nazareth, including Jesus' brothers who didn't believe in Him at first (John 7:5), are in this group. They seriously doubt, but are at least *open* to believing. Jesus' brothers eventually were persuaded.

The third group is people who believe but are plagued by ongoing doubts. The man who cried, "Lord, I believe; help thou mine unbelief" (Mark 9:24 KJV) is in this category. They sincerely *want* to believe, but know they aren't there yet. Unfortunately, they rarely receive a miracle.

The fourth group is people who believe and often "ask in faith, nothing wavering," so receive answers to prayer. But sometimes, when tested, they give in to doubts, and "he that wavereth is like a wave of the sea. . .let not that man think that he shall receive any thing of the Lord" (James 1:6–7 KJV).

The fifth group is people who persevere when tested. They know God's character and are persuaded that He will keep His promises, so determine to trust Him, even if it involves a protracted fight. "I know whom I have believed, and am persuaded that he is able" (2 Timothy 1:12 KJV).

The sixth group is people with great faith. The centurion of Caesarea is in this category (Luke 7:9). The persistent Canaanite woman also belongs here. Jesus said, "O woman, great is your faith! Let it be to you as you desire" (Matthew 15:28 NKJV). Their answers to prayer are often instantaneous.

33. If I'm not certain that God will answer my prayer, what should I do?

It's wonderful when you pray and you're sure that your prayer will be answered. You absolutely *know* it. But it can be frustrating at times to realize that you don't have definite faith. . . yet. You believe in God and believe that He answers prayer, but you can't say that you have a settled peace that *this* particular prayer will be answered.

Often the reason you lack faith is because you're not entirely sure that it's God's will to grant a request. So first pray for Him to show you whether what you desire is within His will. As you begin to believe that God wishes to answer a request, your faith increases. Then you can pray with confidence. However, you still may not have the faith to believe that your prayers will be answered immediately. So *keep* praying.

Great men and women of the past often had full faith the instant they prayed that God had granted their request. But many times, although they believed something was God's will, they prayed and prayed and *kept* praying in faith until they finally received that strong confidence, that sense of assurance that their prayers *had* been heard and *had* been answered. In either case, they believed that God was willing.

Hudson Taylor (1832–1905) was a missionary in China for fifty-one years, and founded the China Inland Mission. One day when Hudson was eighteen years old and his mother was away, he entered his father's library and read a gospel tract. He was so convicted that he gave his heart to Christ. When his mother returned, Hudson told her the news. She said, "I already know. Ten days ago, the very date on which you tell me you read that tract, I spent the entire afternoon in prayer for you until the Lord assured me that my wayward son had been brought into the fold."

34. Should I thank God for answering before I see evidence of it?

If you truly believe when you thank Him, then yes, you should definitely thank Him. George Müller and the three hundred orphans under his care once thanked God for breakfast when they were sitting at the table, yet there was no food in the building. But no sooner did they finish praying when a local baker arrived with enough fresh bread for everyone. On top of that, a milkman's cart broke down outside the orphanage just then, so he decided to donate his ten large cans of milk.

The Bible says, "But my God shall supply all your need according to his riches in glory by Christ Jesus" (Philippians 4:19 KJV). If you have a need, and you pray and trust God to supply, then you count it done and thank Him. If a trusted, faithful friend said he'd give you something you needed, you'd count it done and thank *him* at that point, right?

However, you shouldn't make such a strong affirmation if you don't really believe. You can't hope that God will give you brownie points for brave words that you don't mean. But single-mindedly focusing on the power of God can inspire faith. So if you honestly can't say, "Lord, thank You that You've answered my prayer," you can begin by thanking Him for His awesome power, thanking Him that He's *able* to answer prayer, and that He's *willing* to answer. Focus on these things consistently and you'll eventually find that you *do* have the faith that He will meet your need. Then thank Him for doing so.

You want to end up to point where you can sincerely say, "Thank You, God, for answering my prayer!" If you're not quite there yet, then each time you repeat your request, say, "Thank You that You *will* answer," or "Thank You that You *are* answering."

35. Why do I need to have faith? Can't others who have faith pray for me?

In the answer to question 23, it says: "With a few rare exceptions, we cannot depend on others to have faith *for* us or to pray to God *for* us. However, it's a perfectly sound prayer principle to request other Christians to pray *with* us."

God expects *us* to have faith in matters that concern us personally. When two blind men asked Jesus to heal them, He asked them, "'Do you believe that I am able to do this?' 'Yes, Lord,' they replied. Then He touched their eyes and said, 'According to *your* faith let it be done to you' "—and their sight was restored (Matthew 9:28–30 NIV, emphasis added).

There are reasons why we must have faith ourselves. One is that we must have a personal connection with God. We can't go through life always depending on others to pray for us. Often we'll be in situations where we can't contact others in time. So for our own good, we need to have faith that God answers prayer. We need to mature in Christ.

Also, often the reason we find ourselves in difficulties, have health issues, experience financial problems, and so on, is that God is dealing with us about attitudes or habits that we need to change. We must pray and get right with God before He will answer *anyone's* prayer for us.

On the other hand, sometimes godly people have faith for ordinary miracles, but have outstanding life problems that they don't quite have faith for. At times, the Holy Spirit will prompt others to pray for them. When God answers, this then strengthens their faith to believe Him more.

PRAYER AND GOD'S WILL

36. Does God promise that I shall receive whatever I pray for?

Jesus said, "Therefore I say to you, whatever things you ask when you pray, believe that you receive them, and you will have them" (Mark 11:24 NKJV). Some people point out that Jesus said that you'll receive "whatever" you pray for—providing you have the faith.

There don't seem to be any conditions attached, which has sometimes led Christians to pray for sinful, selfish things. C. H. Spurgeon was a preacher known for his deep emphasis on God's grace and love and mercy, yet he bluntly stated, "Ah, my brethren, we little know how many of our prayers are an abomination to the Lord."

Even though there don't appear to be any conditions other than the need for faith, there are indeed conditions. The primary one is that we must pray within God's will. "Now this is the confidence that we have in Him, that if we ask anything *according to His will*, He hears us. And if we know that He hears us, whatever we ask, we know that we have the petitions that we have asked of Him" (1 John 5:14–15 NKJV, emphasis added). Also, we must obey God: "And whatever we ask we receive from Him, *because* we keep His commandments and do those things that are pleasing in His sight" (1 John 3:22 NKJV, emphasis added).

Notice the striking similarity between these three passages. All proclaim the certainty of answered prayer: Mark 11:24 says that "whatever things you ask. . .you will have," 1 John 5:15 says that "whatever we ask, we know that we have," and 1 John 3:22 says, "whatever we ask we receive." They are clearly different facets of the same powerful message.

It's unreasonable, therefore, to pluck Mark 11:24 out of context and use it as a stand-alone prayer principle. Certainly faith is vital, but it must be understood in the context of other closely related scriptures.

37. How can I know what God's will is, so I can pray for the right thing?

The most important step in discovering God's will is to sincerely *desire* His will. This may seem obvious, but by nature people seek security and comfort and avoid insecurity and hardships. So often when we say we're seeking *God's* will, we're actually presenting *our* desires to Him and seeking His approval. Even Jesus acknowledged that He wanted to avoid dying on the cross, though He knew it was His Father's will. But He prayed, "Not My will, but Yours, be done" (Luke 22:42 NKJV).

Proverbs 3:6 (NLT) says, "Seek his will in all you do, and he will show you which path to take." It's easier to find God's will in uncertain, complex situations if we're already following His will in obvious everyday choices. Much of the time we *know* what's right because we've read it in His Word (Romans 2:18).

Seeking God's will also can mean seeking the wisdom to choose between various options. If we're not set on our own desires but are open to what God wants, we're more apt to make the right choice. Like Jesus, we must sincerely seek the will of the Father (John 5:30). Our heavenly Father may give us the desires of our heart, or He may require us to surrender them. The American evangelist D. L. Moody said, "Spread out your petition before God, and then say, 'Thy will, not mine, be done.' The sweetest lesson I have learned in God's school is to let the Lord choose for me."

A final thought: if we spent more time praying for God to change us and make us more like Jesus, we'd spend less time praying for selfish things that aren't His will, and less time wondering why those prayers aren't answered.

38. Doesn't God promise to give me the desires of my heart?

A Christian proverb states, "God promises to supply all our needs, not all our wants." There's truth to this. In Philippians 4:19 (KJV) Paul wrote, "But my God shall supply all your need." He went on to define what *his* needs were: "But if we have food and clothing, we will be content with that" (1 Timothy 6:8 NIV). Now, Paul was a single, itinerant preacher who had "no certain dwellingplace" (1 Corinthians 4:11 KJV), so he kept his list short.

Most of us in the West have a much larger list of what constitutes a need. Among these are items that many people in the world consider a luxury. But God oftentimes *does* give us things that aren't absolutely essential. After all, scripture says: "Delight yourself also in the LORD, and He shall give you the desires of your heart" (Psalm 37:4 NKJV).

Christians often quote this verse when praying for a husband or a wife—and normally that's a legitimate desire God delights to give us. (And He gives us *choice* in this matter—see Numbers 36:6 and 1 Corinthians 7:39.) But some of us go on to insist that He give us other wishes of our overly desirous hearts, including affluent lifestyles, expensive vacations, opulent homes, luxury cars, and so on. D. L. Moody wrote, "We must have a warrant for our prayers. If we have some great desire, we must search the scriptures to find if it be right to ask it."

There is, in fact, a condition attached

to this promise: we are first and foremost to delight ourselves in the Lord. If we truly do that, we'll desire things that *God* desires for us—and He may reveal to us that many things *we* desire aren't actually best for us. For example, although riches aren't wrong in themselves, Jesus warned that "the deceitfulness of riches, and the lusts of other things entering in" tend to choke out the Word of God in our lives (Mark 4:19 KJV).

39. Didn't Jesus say He came to give us "the abundant life"?

Jesus said, "I am the door. If anyone enters by Me, he will be saved, and will go in and out and find pasture. . . . I have come that they may have life, and that they may have it more abundantly" (John 10:9–10 NKJV).

"The Abundant Life" doctrine says that it's God's will for Christians to prosper financially—that being poor is His curse, while wealth is a distinct sign of His blessing. Now, Jesus did come to give us life abundantly, but He's talking about salvation here; the green pasture isn't dollar bills, but spiritual blessings.

What about Deuteronomy 28:1–13 where God promised to bless His people materially if they obeyed Him? When God promises to bless with plenty, it means He will supply all our need. These verses are *not* a guarantee that we will be wealthy and overflowing with material things.

In the centuries before Jesus, Asaph saw "the prosperity of the wicked" and realized that it was the covetous who often prospered inordinately: "Their eyes bulge with abundance; they have more than heart could wish" and "they increase in riches" (Psalm 73:3, 7, 12 NKJV). Paul said to turn away from those who suppose that "gain is godliness," but added that "godliness with contentment is great gain" (1 Timothy 6:5–6 KJV).

In Jesus' day, "the common people heard him gladly" (Mark 12:37 KJV). These people were mostly lower middle class or poor, at least by American standards. Yet Jesus said, "Blessed are you poor, for yours is the kingdom of God" (Luke 6:20 NKJV). And they *were* blessed. They didn't have everything we today have, but they were content, and therefore had great gain.

Poverty is certainly not an ideal state, nor is it wrong to prosper. However, the Bible cautions that "those who desire to be rich fall into temptation and a snare" (1 Timothy 6:9 NKJV), and admonishes, "If riches increase, do not set your heart on them" (Psalm 62:10 NKJV).

40. Will God give me something that isn't good for me if I insist on it?

Sometimes, yes. In Numbers chapter 11, God had just finished providing manna for the children of Israel. They should've been satisfied. Instead, they began to lament, "Who will give us meat to eat?" (verse 4). They longed for the fish they'd once enjoyed, and were so bitter about its lack that they wished they'd never left Egypt—even though they'd been slaves there.

Moses told them, "Therefore the Lord will give you meat, and you shall eat. . .for a whole month, until it comes out of your nostrils and becomes loathsome to you" (Numbers 11:18, 20 NKJV). Psalms declares, "But they. . .did not wait for his plan to unfold. In the desert they gave in to their craving. . . . So he gave them what they asked for, but sent a wasting disease among them" (Psalm 106:13–15 NIV). Or, as the New King James version says, "He gave them their request, but sent leanness into their soul" (Psalm 106:15 NKJV).

Sometimes God gives us what we insist on, even though it's not what He desires for us. He does this because we've rejected His will, and the thing we're insisting upon will serve to teach us a lesson that we're not willing to learn any other way. Have you ever longed and prayed for something and, when you finally got it, found that it left you empty? Yet you were stuck with it—at least until you repented. How could this be God's will? Well, when we disobey Him, He has promised to chastise us. Disobedience brings judgment. But remember, for Christians, God's "judgment" is actually discipline. It has a loving purpose. "Those whom I love I rebuke and discipline. So be earnest and repent" (Revelation 3:19 NIV).

A Christian proverb states, "Be careful what you pray for. You might actually get it." That's because, along with getting it, you may also get leanness in your soul.

41. If I pray hard enough, can I change God's mind?

No, you can't—although, as the last question stated, in certain cases when you reject God's will, He gives you what you ask for to teach you clearly that it doesn't satisfy. But if God has determined to do something, you can't pray He will change His mind and do something "better." Yet, you may argue, there are scriptures where God declared that He'd do something but a man of God interceded in prayer and, so it seems, actually changed His mind.

For example, God stated that He'd determined to destroy Sodom and Gomorrah (Genesis 18:20–23), and in Genesis 19:17–22 (NIV), an angel urged Lot to flee to the mountains lest he be swept away in the destruction. Lot pleaded to flee into Zoar instead. The angel said, "Very well, I will grant this request too; I will not overthrow the town you speak of." Did Lot change God's mind? No. God had only sworn to overthrow Sodom and Gomorrah. It was within His will for Zoar to be spared. But if Lot *hadn't* asked, it too would have been destroyed.

In 2 Kings 20:1–6 (NIV), Hezekiah was sick and wondered if he'd recover. God sent Isaiah to tell him: "You are going to die; you will not recover." But when Hezekiah prayed, God sent Isaiah back saying, "I have heard your prayer and seen your tears; I will heal you." Did Hezekiah change God's mind? No. God hadn't irrevocably decided that he had to die. It was *always* within His will for Hezekiah to be healed. . .but if he hadn't prayed, he would've died.

God threatened to destroy Nineveh, but when its people repented, He didn't destroy it. The reason? God takes no pleasure in the death of the wicked. He longs for them to repent (Ezekiel 33:11). He is "a gracious and compassionate God, slow to anger and abounding in love, a God who relents from sending calamity" (Jonah 4:2 NIV). God has predetermined that He will relent from judgment if His people repent and earnestly pray (see 2 Chronicles 7:13 –14).

42. If I pray for someone to become a Christian, will it happen?

If you stress predestination, you may conclude that it's only worth praying for those whom God has destined to receive salvation—and that if they do receive Christ, it's because it was God's will all along. If you stress free will, you may protest that God doesn't override human choices and "make" anyone become a Christian. The most He'd do is present then with repeated opportunities to receive His mercy.

Whatever the case, God commands us to pray for the lost. Paul said, "I urge, then, first of all, that petitions, prayers, intercession and thanksgiving be made for all people. . . . This is good, and pleases God our Savior, who wants all people to be saved and to come to a knowledge of the truth" (1 Timothy 2:1, 3–4 NIV). God wants *all* people to be saved, so it's His will that we pray for them. And down through history, Christians have devoted themselves to such prayers.

George Müller is an outstanding example. One day, he began to pray for five of his friends. He had such faith that this was God's will that he said, "I hope in God, I pray on, and look yet for the answer. They are not converted yet, but they will be." After some months, one of them became a Christian—but it took ten more years for two more to be saved. The fourth man was saved twenty-five years after Müller began praying. The fifth man resisted God, but Müller never gave up. He prayed fifty-two years for him and died without seeing him converted. Just after Müller's funeral, however, the man gave his heart to Christ.

D. L. Moody added, "So if you are anxious about the conversion of some relative, or some friend, make up your mind that you will give God no rest, day or night, till He grants your petition."

43. What part does the Holy Spirit play in prayer?

Christians believe that one of the purposes of the Holy Spirit living in our hearts is to empower us to live Jesus' commands. This is true. In addition, the same indwelling Spirit prompts us, stirring up our hearts and reminding us of the need to pray. C. H. Spurgeon stated, "Prayer is an art which only the Spirit can teach us. He is the giver of all prayer." Finally, if we have faith when we pray, God then sends the Spirit to answer our prayers. So the Holy Spirit is involved with our prayers from beginning to end.

In addition, the Bible states: "For we do not know what we should pray for as we ought, but the Spirit Himself makes intercession for us with groanings which cannot be uttered. . . . He makes intercession for the saints according to the will of God" (Romans 8:26–27 NKJV). Paul also wrote that "no one can know God's thoughts except God's own Spirit" (1 Corinthians 2:11 NLT). So if we want to pray for things that are God's will, our prayers must be inspired by the Holy Spirit.

What are these "groanings which cannot be uttered"? You may have experienced times when you were so overwhelmed that you could scarcely speak. In the Bible, "Hannah was in deep anguish, crying bitterly as she prayed to the Lord" (1 Samuel 1:10, 13 NLT). The evangelist George Whitefield said, "Thus Hannah prayed, when she spoke not aloud, only her lips moved. . . . This is what the apostle means by the 'Spirit making intercession with groanings which cannot be uttered.' "

And as C. H. Spurgeon pointed out, "Groanings which cannot be uttered are often prayers which cannot be refused."

CLAIMING GOD'S PROMISES

44. What does it mean to "claim God's promises"?

In the Bible, God made several specific promises to Abraham (see Genesis 12:2–3; 15:4–6; 17:15–19). To his credit, Abraham believed. God also made a covenant with the nation of Israel, and promised to bless them if they kept His commandments (see Deuteronomy 28:1–13). If they faithfully obeyed Him, they had the right to claim the blessings God had promised.

God also promised He'd send a Savior to save humanity. Peter said, "For the promise is to you and to. . .as many as the Lord our God will call" (Acts 2:39 NKJV). God has promised us salvation, and we may claim this for ourselves. Years later, Peter wrote that there "have been given to us exceedingly great and precious promises, that through these you may be partakers of the divine nature" (2 Peter 1:4 NKJV). But we must take *hold* of these promises. We must lay claim to them being fulfilled in *our* lives.

Our heavenly Father has also made promises related to our physical well-being. For example, an oft-quoted verse states, "But my God shall supply all your need according to his riches in glory by Christ Jesus" (Philippians 4:19 KJV). We can claim this promise during time of need and request that God fulfill it in our life.

God has made many promises in the Bible, but until we lay claim to them, they won't do us any good. We must appropriate them. To appropriate means "to lay hold on; to claim for one's own." In modern English, it usually means "to take something for your own use, especially without permission." But it can *also* mean to take something for your use *with* permission—as is the case with God's Word.

And remember that "faith is the. . .title deed" (Hebrews 11:1 AMP). When you wish to claim a piece of property, you simply present the title deed as evidence that it's yours.

45. Does God sometimes personalize Bible promises to me?

Yes. Sometimes you'll be involved in things that tax your abilities, your resources, your wisdom, or your faith. But as you read the Bible, you are sometimes led to a verse that seems to speak directly to your situation. It electrifies your spirit, and you know that this is God's promise to you, so you claim for Him to fulfill it in your life—and He does. God can personalize a promise to you, even though it was made to a specific Bible individual or was originally made in a different context.

Sometimes God will bring a Bible verse to your memory while you're praying. Jesus promised that "the Holy Spirit. . .will teach you all things, and bring to your remembrance all things that I said to you" (John 14:26 NKJV). The words He speaks to your heart are His promise to you.

Sometimes you'll be in middle of Bible reading, when God will highlight a verse. It may be a passage you've read many times before, but this time it seems to jump out at you. It's as if you're seeing it for the first time.

"Open my eyes, that I may see wondrous things from Your law" (Psalm 119:18 NKJV).

Other times, you might simply open your Bible, after praying desperately, and your eyes will fall on the one verse in the entire Bible that addresses *exactly* what you're going through. This is known as "cutting your Bible," and though it definitely shouldn't be done lightly or as a regular practice, it has been known to supply miraculous guidance.

In many of these cases, the verse that God leads you to may not even be a Bible promise per se—simply a statement of fact. But because God uses it to speak directly into your situation, it becomes His personal promise to you.

46. How does it help my prayers to memorize verses from the Bible?

It's important to read God's Word so that you know exactly what He has promised to do. And obviously, it's important to *remember* what it says. Some people recall passages because they've read them so often. Other Christians not only read scriptures often, but commit them to memory, repeating the verses over and over until they know them by heart. Then they have these promises in their memory and can quote them in times of need.

God told the Israelites, "You shall lay up these words of mine in your heart and in your soul" (Deuteronomy 11:18 NKJV). Jesus Himself memorized passages of the Bible. We know this because during a time of severe testing, He was able to quote these verses verbatim to counter Satan's lies (see Matthew 4:1–11).

When praying, it can be very helpful to quote portions of the scriptures. Some people think that the purpose of this is to "quote the contract" to remind God what He has promised and insist that He honor His Word. Rather, it's mostly to remind *ourselves* of what He said. When we're reminded that our Father has made a promise, that we have a basis for our claim, it inspires our faith and gives us authority in our prayers.

For example, when praying for finances, you might quote Philippians 4:19 then say, "Dear God, You promised in Your Word that You'd supply *all* my needs. I trust You now to do that." Or when praying for healing, you might remember Exodus 15:26 (NLT) and pray, "Father, Your Word says, 'I am the LORD who heals you,' so I claim healing now, in Jesus' name."

C. H. Spurgeon said, "A mighty piece of weaponry in the battle of prayer is God's promise."

47. Should we demand or insist that God has to keep His promises?

When heading to distant Africa, David Livingstone was encouraged by the scripture "lo, I am with you always, even unto the end of the world" (Matthew 28:20 KJV). He knew that whatever danger he faced, God had promised to be with him. So he confidently stated, "That is a promise I can rely upon, for it is the word of a gentleman of honor." Again and again, when facing very real danger, he remembered this verse and reminded himself, "It is the word of a gentleman of the most strict and sacred honor!"

In those days, in Victorian England, a "gentleman" was a man of considerable standing in society, and because he valued his good reputation, a true gentleman always kept his word. And Livingstone was right: God is a gentleman of honor.

Some people, however, become frustrated when God doesn't answer prayer quickly and they must repeatedly ask Him for something. When they pray, they act as if God is a cheap landlord who has to be pestered before he will finally fix the leaky roof. They remind God that His reputation is on the line, so He *must* honor His contract. Others act as if they're dealing with a crooked builder who didn't fulfill his obligations, and who must be "taken to court" before he'll finally, reluctantly make things good. They hold their finger on a verse and get in God's face. When they "come boldly" unto His throne (Hebrews 4:16 KJV) it's often an unpleasant confrontation. How sad!

Livingstone was right, however: God is a gentleman of honor. He will make good His word because He *is* good and because He cares (Matthew 7:11). There are reasons why He sometimes delays answering prayer, and we'll address those in a later section.

48. Has God made a covenant and promised to always answer our prayers?

Many Christians believe that God has made a binding covenant and is under obligation to answer their prayers. They can therefore declare what they want Him to do, so long as they declare in faith. In their view, God doesn't necessarily keep His word because He's a gentleman. He keeps His word because it's a binding contract and He has *no choice* but to honor it.

There is a significant difference between this doctrine—emphatic as it is—and the extremes to which some in the Word Faith movement take it. They teach that when Adam and Eve were created in the image of God (Genesis 1:27) they were literally gods. God merely spoke the word and Creation came into being (Psalm 33:6, 9), and humans were given this same authority. They lost it when they fell, but we regained it in Christ.

Word Faith proclaims a principle called "the force of faith" or "faith-force." Based on verses such as, "Death and life are in the power of the tongue" (Proverbs 18:21 NKJV), they stress the importance of "positive declarations." According to this doctrine, God has set up the cause-and-effect mechanics of spiritual principles, and He Himself operates completely within the bounds of these laws. He *must* give them whatever they demand.

One of the problems with this teaching is that it reduces God to a genie in a lamp, theirs to command. Also, its mechanical view of prayer undermines an understanding of God as Father. Daniel was a great prophet, yet he didn't command God. Yes, he reminded Him of His covenant, but prayed, "O Lord, great and awesome God, who keeps His covenant and mercy with those who love Him. . .we do not present our supplications before You because of our righteous deeds, but because of Your great mercies" (Daniel 9:4,18 NKJV).

49. Can Christians command God to answer their prayers?

Some Christians believe that they have the authority to *command* God to do a miracle. They quote this verse: "Thus saith the Lord. . .

Ask me of things to come concerning my sons, and concerning the work of my hands command ye me" (Isaiah 45:11 KJV). However, the New International Version reads: "This is what the Lord says. . .do you question me about my children, or give me orders about the work of my hands?" Verse 9 clarifies who God was rebuking: "Woe to those who quarrel with their Maker." They *try* to command God, but are in no position to do so.

However, when Jesus rebuked the wind and said to the waves, 'Silence! Be still!' the storm stopped, and the disciples marveled, "Even the wind and waves obey him!" (Mark 4:39, 41 NLT). It may stretch your faith to learn this, but Jesus also gave *us* authority over things. After all, He stated, "You can say to this mulberry tree, 'Be pulled up by the roots and be planted in the sea,' and it would obey you" (Luke 17:6 NKJV). If you have great faith, mulberry trees have to obey you. God does *not*.

Charles Stanley says in *The Wonderful Spirit Filled Life* (1992), "The Holy Spirit's power cannot be harnessed. His power cannot be used to accomplish anything other than the Father's will. He is not a candy dispenser. He is not a vending machine. He is not a genie waiting for someone to rub His lamp the right way. He is holy God."

You're simply not authorized to command God to do a miracle. However, when praying for healing, for example, you *can* quote a Bible promise then state, "Body, I command you, in Jesus' name, line up with the Word of God! I command you to obey the will of God! Be healed!" That in itself is a bold prayer, but if you have mulberry-tree faith, God will bless it.

50. Can we command a miracle to happen rather than asking God to do it?

Some Christians don't pray for God to do a miracle. They believe that He's already placed His power at their disposal, under *their* authority, and that all they have to do is release it. Luke says, "Then he called his twelve disciples together, and gave them power and authority over all devils, and to cure diseases" (Luke 9:1 KJV). It's pointed out that Jesus didn't tell them to pray for *God* to heal, but said, "Heal the sick" (Matthew 10:8 KJV). In other words: *you* do it.

To back up this claim, people point out that when Peter saw the lame man in the Temple, he said, "Silver and gold I do not have, but *what I do have* I give you: In the name of Jesus Christ of Nazareth, rise up and walk" (Acts 3:6 NKJV, emphasis added). And when Paul saw the lame man in the city of Lystra, he simply shouted, "Stand up straight on your feet!" (Acts 14:10 NKJV).

Nevertheless, these startling declarations must be understood in context. God is still the one who does the miracles, and Christians must still pray for Him to do them. Before they publicly commanded miracles to happen, the apostles spent hours on their knees imploring God: "O Sovereign Lord, Creator of heaven and earth. . . Stretch out your hand with healing power; may miraculous signs and wonders be done" (Acts 4:24, 29–30 NLT). As a *result*, "through the hands of the apostles many signs and wonders were done among the people" (Acts 5:12 NKJV).

Also note that when Tabitha died, Peter first

"knelt down and prayed." *Then* "turning to the body he said, 'Tabitha arise'" (Acts 9:40 NKJV).

So how does this principle work? As D. L. Moody observed, "A man who prays much in private will make short prayers in public."

FAITH FOR HEALING

51. Does Jesus still miraculously heal people in this modern day?

All Christian denominations believe that God can heal the sick, even today. However, many people question whether this is something that He does often or consistently. Even believers who are skeptical about the claims of faith healers believe, in principle, that God can heal. . .*if* He's willing.

On the other hand, a growing number of Christians readily turn to miraculous healing when sick. Since "Jesus Christ is the same yesterday, today, and forever" (Hebrews 13:8 NLT), they reason that He still heals the way He did when He traveled around Judea and Galilee. Some go further, pointing out that Jesus "healed them all" (Matthew 12:15; Luke 6:19 NKJV), so claim that it's *always* His will to heal *everyone* today.

Whatever your belief, we can agree that

if we spent more time seeking God for healing and had more faith, we'd see more miracles. And yes, people *are* still being healed in countries around the world today. If it's not happening often in the church you attend, talk to Christians from other churches. Even people in your own church may have experienced miraculous healings. Ask around and find out. You might be greatly encouraged by some of the miracles great and small that you hear about.

F. F. Bosworth wrote in his 1924 book, *Christ the Healer*, "Appropriating faith is not believing that God can but that He will. Those who claim to believe in healing, but say one word in favor of it and ten words against it, cannot produce faith for healing."

52. Does God give certain Christians specific gifts of divine healing?

Yes, definitely. Jesus gave His twelve apostles "power and authority. . .to cure diseases" (Luke 9:1 KJV). "After these things the Lord appointed seventy others also" and instructed them to "heal the sick" (Luke 10:1, 9 NKJV). These individuals had divinely appointed authority for healing. But does God intend for only select people to have power over sickness? Or has He given *all* believers authority for healing?

The Bible also says: "And these signs will follow those who believe: In My name they will cast out demons; they will. . .lay hands on the sick, and they will recover" (Mark 16:17–18 NKJV). It's clear therefore—that potentially at least—Jesus extended this healing authority to *all* believers.

Nevertheless, whenever the New Testament describes healing miracles, it states that they were done either by apostles, elders, or deacons (see Acts 5:12–16; 8:5–7; James 5:14–15). When a Christian named Tabitha became sick and died, the Christians of Joppa weren't able to heal her or to raise her from the dead—so they sent for the apostle Peter; and when he prayed, God did the miracle (Acts 9:36–41).

Paul asked the following rhetorical questions: "Are all apostles? Are all prophets? Are all teachers? Are all workers of miracles? Do all have gifts of healings?" (1 Corinthians

12:29–30 NKJV). The answer in each case is no. Certain individuals have remarkable, unique gifts of healing.

But the good news is that even if you don't have an *outstanding* anointing for healing, the same power of Jesus is available to you. You might not see as many instantaneous miracles—perhaps you'll have to persevere in prayer—but God has given us *all* a measure of faith. And that faith can be used to receive a miracle of healing as readily as any other kind of answer to prayer.

53. Does Isaiah 53:5 give all believers authority to claim healing?

Many Christians say that all believers have full authority for healing, and should expect it as part of Christ's atonement. This is because Isaiah 53 prophesies about Jesus, and Isaiah 53:5 (NKJV) says that "by His stripes we are healed." It's believed that although Jesus' blood was shed to save our spirits, His body suffered stripes to heal *our* bodies.

In the Lord's Supper, Jesus gave His

disciples bread (His body) and wine (His blood), but only stated that His blood was necessary for salvation (Matthew 26:26–28). Why then do we partake of His body, if not for our physical healing?

God does heal our bodies, however, Isaiah 53:5 is *not* a promise to do so. No place in the New Testament do Christians quote this when praying for healing. When the apostles healed "every disease and sickness" (Matthew 10:1 NIV), they did so with the authority Christ had given them, and "in the name of Jesus Christ" (Acts 3:6 NIV).

Isaiah 53:5 is talking about forgiveness of sin: "But He was *wounded* for our *transgressions*, He was *bruised* for our *iniquities*; the *chastisement* for our *peace* was upon Him, and by His *stripes* we are *healed*" (Isaiah 53:5 NKJV, emphasis added). Peter referred to this when he said, "by whose stripes you were healed" (1 Peter 2:24 NKJV). He was addressing believers (hence he said "were healed"), and a careful reading of 1 Peter 2:21–25 shows that he was talking about salvation, not physical healing.

Why then did Jesus tell us to partake of His body (the bread) if only His blood was necessary for salvation? Because His blood was not primarily shed from the nail holes in His hands and feet. When whipped by a *flagellum*, Jesus' body was so savagely lacerated that His arteries were sliced open and His blood poured rapidly from many deep wounds (stripes). He was suffering hypovolemic shock from severe blood loss long before He was nailed to the cross. He endured all that to save us.

54. What gives Christians authority to receive healing?

You may wonder, "If God didn't intend me to quote Isaiah 53:5 when praying for healing, what *does* He give me authority for?" Please reread questions 3, 4, and 5. Our authority rests in the fact that the all-powerful Spirit of Jesus dwells in our hearts, and if we're submitted to Him and praying within His will, we can present our petitions with His authority in His name. And the Bible is clear is that God heals us:

- "I am the LORD who heals you" (Exodus 15:26 NLT).

- "And the LORD will take away from you all sickness, and will afflict you with none of the terrible diseases of Egypt" (Deuteronomy 7:15 NKJV).

- "Bless the LORD, O my soul. . .who forgives all your iniquities, who heals all your diseases" (Psalm 103:2–3 NKJV).

- "He sent out his word and healed them; he rescued them from the grave" (Psalm 107:20 NIV).

- "Now a leper came. . .saying to Him, 'If You are willing, You can make me clean.' Then Jesus, moved with compassion, stretched out His hand and touched him, and said to him, 'I am willing; be cleansed' " (Mark 1:40–41 NKJV).

- "He [Jesus]. . .healed all the sick. This was to fulfill what was spoken through the prophet Isaiah: 'He took up our infirmities and bore our diseases' " (Matthew 8:16–17 NIV).

- "And these signs will follow those who believe: In My name they will. . .lay hands on the sick, and they will recover" (Mark 16:17–18 NKJV).

- "Are any of you sick? You should call for the elders of the church to come and pray over you, anointing you with oil in the name of the Lord. Such a prayer offered in faith will heal the sick, and the Lord will make you well" (James 5:14–15 NLT).

Read these promises repeatedly. Meditate upon them. Quote them when you pray for healing. Read the Gospels to remind yourself of Jesus' healing miracles, and remember that "Jesus Christ is the same yesterday, today, and forever" (Hebrews 13:8 NLT).

55. Does God always heal obedient, righteous Christians?

There's a deep appeal in thinking that healing is part of the atonement, literally guaranteed to believers. The Abundant Life doctrine takes this even further, saying that God's will for Christians is not only perfect health but abundant wealth. Word Faith doctrine likewise states that God is obligated to give us whatever we declare, including healing.

However, there's a huge downside to such beliefs. Millions of godly believers sincerely pray for healing but continue to suffer from chronic illnesses. They then conclude that they must not be very spiritual. Others who attempt to "speak a miracle into existence" for a terminally ill loved one are often devastated when that person dies. They then question the faithfulness of God, since, after all, He supposedly "promised" to always heal.

While it's true that we often don't receive healing because we lack faith or we're disobedient, the fact is that God does *not* invariably heal. Paul, who had outstanding healing gifts, couldn't heal a faithful coworker, but wrote, "Trophimus have I left at Miletum sick" (2 Timothy 4:20 KJV). Timothy had "frequent illnesses" of the stomach. Unable to heal him, Paul wrote him practical advice (1 Timothy 5:23 NIV). Paul himself had a "thorn in the flesh" that he couldn't get rid of, despite praying repeatedly (2 Corinthians 12:7 KJV).

Elisha had faith for astonishing miracles, but 2 Kings 13:14 (NKJV) tells us that "Elisha had become sick with the illness of which he would die." Yet there was such a powerful anointing on Elisha that, even after he became ill and died, a dead man was raised back to life when he came in contact with Elisha's bones (2 Kings 13:21). Try figuring *that* one out.

God can heal and does heal, and does so in response to the faith-filled prayers of those who obey Him. But there are times, we don't always know why, when He refrains from doing healing miracles.

56. What was Paul's "thorn in the flesh" and what was its purpose?

Many Bible scholars believe that Paul's "thorn in the flesh" was an eye disease called chronic ophthalmia. This is an inflammation of the membranes or the coats of the eye or eyeball. While not normally painful, the yellow excretions would have made him unpleasant to look at. Paul commended the Galatians that they didn't treat him with contempt despite his illness—but would've given him their own eyes had it been possible (Galatians 4:13–15). Paul often wrote in "large letters" because of his poor eyesight (Galatians 6:11 NLT).

Why did God give him such a disease, and not let him get rid of it? After describing being taken up to heaven, Paul said, "I have received such wonderful revelations from God. So to keep me from becoming proud, I was given a thorn in my flesh, a messenger from Satan to torment me and keep me from becoming proud. Three different times I begged the Lord to take it away. Each time he said, " 'My grace is all you need. My power works best in weakness' " (2 Corinthians 12:7–9 NLT).

If you suffer from a chronic illness or handicap, it might be your "thorn in the flesh." But do not automatically assume this is the case. Very often God simply requires us to persevere in prayer over stubborn illnesses. If He doesn't heal you right away, it doesn't necessarily mean He wants you to *remain* unhealed. After all, if we believe that it's *not* God's will for us to be healed, then why do we continue to seek after operations or remedies to alleviate our illness? It God desires that we remain sick, why seek natural cures?

The psalmist said, "It is good for me that I have been afflicted; that I might learn thy statutes" (Psalm 119:71 KJV). Even if God *allows* you to be afflicted, it doesn't need to be permanent. Often you can be healed after you learn your lesson.

57. Does the devil cause all sickness and disease?

Paul stated that his affliction was caused by "a messenger from Satan" (2 Corinthians 12:7 KJV), and Jesus repeatedly cast out demons that were causing sicknesses or handicaps. In one case, an evil spirit had entered a boy, not only rendering him deaf and mute, but causing destructive convulsions. When Jesus cast the spirit out, the boy was instantly healed (Mark 9:17–27).

In most cases, however, Jesus healed the multitudes *without* casting evil spirits from them. Does this mean that the devil wasn't the cause of most sickness? In one sense, it almost doesn't matter. The bottom line is: Jesus Christ has power over sicknesses and diseases, whether they're caused by evil spirits or contagious viruses, whether they're genetic or the result of an accident or unhealthy lifestyle.

Nevertheless, the Bible tells us that Jesus "went about doing good, and healing all that were oppressed of the devil" (Acts 10:38 KJV). One "daughter of Abraham" had been "bound" by Satan for eighteen years (Luke 13:16 KJV).

The implication is that, although demons rarely possessed people, they nevertheless oppressed them by causing them to get sick. Scripture indicates that they can only do so with God's permission (Job 2:1–7), and that often—but not always—they gain permission as a result of sin (Psalm 107:17–20; John 9:1–3).

But what about hereditary illnesses or diseases like cancer? Are they always the work of demons? Are they *always* caused by sin? Bear in mind that fungi, bacteria, viruses, viroids, phytoplasmas, protozoa, and nematodes cause various diseases in plants in every corner of the world. Do demons spend a vast portion of their time spreading fungi and viroids in millions of square miles of distant, uninhabited forests? It hardly seems likely.

It seems more credible that a great proportion of diseases in the world—whether in plants, animals, or people—are a result of the fact that we live in a fallen world. And the good news is: God can restore health no matter *what* has caused its lack.

58. Is it important to lay hands on people when we pray for their healing?

When Jesus was in Capernaum and the crowds brought sick people, "he laid his hands on every one of them, and healed them" (Luke 4:40 KJV). Jesus promised, "And these signs shall follow them that believe. . .they shall lay hands on the sick, and they shall recover" (Mark 16:17–18 KJV). So this was what Christians did: "Paul went in to him and prayed, and he laid his hands on him and healed him" (Acts 28:8 NKJV).

Jesus is known to have healed at least three people from a distance, without even seeing them (Matthew 8:5–13; Mark 7:24–30; John 4:46–53). But He seems to have frequently physically touched people.

Conversely, on many occasions people touched Jesus to receive healing (Mark 6:56). Why did they feel the need to make physical contact? "The people all tried to touch him, *because power was coming from him* and healing them all" (Luke 6:19 NIV, emphasis added). On one occasion, a woman secretly touched the fringe of His robe. Jesus asked, "Who touched me?" When everyone denied it, Jesus said, "Someone deliberately touched me, for *I felt healing power go out from me*" (Luke 8:45–46 NLT, emphasis added).

God is perfectly capable of healing someone even if we pray from a distance, but the Scriptures are clear that spiritual power is usually more readily imparted when physical contact is made. And this is why many Christians lay hands on someone when praying for them. (See also Acts 8:17; 19:6; 2 Timothy 1:6.)

59. Should we only trust God and not depend on natural means at all?

Some people refer to the following Bible passages as proof that God doesn't like doctors, and that if we're sick, we should *only* look to God for healing: "Asa became diseased in his feet, and his malady was severe; yet in his disease he did not seek the Lord, but the physicians. So Asa. . .died" (2 Chronicles 16:12–13 NKJV). "Now a certain woman had a flow of blood for twelve years, and had suffered many things from many physicians. She had spent all that she had and was no better, but rather grew worse" (Mark 5:25–26 NKJV).

Asa's mistake was not in looking to doctors, but in *only* depending on them and not seeking God no matter how severe his malady became. And while it's true that doctors can mis-diagnose and can't cure some diseases, millions of people benefit daily from the care of the medical profession, including sincere Christian doctors and nurses. As Jesus said, "Healthy people don't need a doctor—sick people do" (Luke 5:31 NLT).

Luke wrote a Gospel and the Book of Acts—nearly 30 percent of the New Testament. He was a doctor when Paul met him in AD 50, and ten years later, was still practicing medicine alongside his missionary work. We know this because in AD 60 Paul referred to him as "Luke the beloved physician" (Colossians 4:14 NKJV).

God sometimes chooses to use medicine and natural remedies in place of outright miracles. When King Hezekiah was dying of a deadly boil and cried out to God, instead of healing Hezekiah miraculously, God inspired the prophet Isaiah to say, "Prepare a poultice of figs and apply it to the boil, and he will recover" (Isaiah 38:21 NIV). And he did!

As Jon Courson wrote in the *Application Commentary Volume 1, Old Testament* (2005), "It's the Lord who heals and He can use any method He chooses."

60. What does "stepping out in faith" mean?

Once you've prayed for healing, some Christians say, "Now you need to step out in faith." What they mean is that if you truly believed that God heard your prayer and healed you then you should put your faith into action. For example, if you believe that God healed your injured foot, you should try to walk on it.

In Matthew 14:22–31, the disciples were crossing the Sea of Galilee when Jesus came walking on the water. At first, they thought it was a ghost, but Jesus assured them it was Him. So Peter said, "Lord, if it is You, command me to come to You on the water" (Matthew 14:28

NKJV). Jesus said, "Come," so Peter stepped out of the boat and began walking on the waves toward Jesus. This was definitely "stepping out in faith."

Another time, Jesus met ten lepers and they begged Him to have mercy on them. The Law of Moses specified that if you were healed of leprosy, you should let priests examine you to make *sure* you'd been cured. So Jesus said, "Go show yourselves to the priests." The lepers ran off, "And *as they went*, they were cleansed" (Luke 17:14 NIV, emphasis added).

D. L. Moody illustrated this principle of expectancy when he said, "If you pray for bread and bring no basket to carry it, you prove the doubting spirit, which may be the only hindrance to the boon you ask." Sometimes you won't actually be healed *until* you step out in faith.

However, before you throw your glasses or crutches away or toss your medicine in the trash, please reread question 34 ("Should I thank God for answering before I see evidence of it?") God can't honor those who *wish* they had faith but actually *don't*. "But without faith it is impossible to please Him" (Hebrews 11:6 NKJV). You genuinely must have faith.

WHEN PRAYERS AREN'T ANSWERED

61. Why does God sometimes not give me what I'm asking for?

There are several possible answers to this question, so let's first look at one of the most obvious reasons: what you're praying for may simply not be God's will. We dealt with this in question 36 ("Does God promise that I shall receive whatever I pray for?") and question 38 ("Doesn't God promise to give me the desires of my heart?"), but let's look at this more closely.

What you're asking for might seem to be a perfectly legitimate request, but God knows you better than you know yourself and is aware of your motives. For example, you might ask Him to bless you financially yet continue to experience a tight budget. The reason might be "when you ask, you do not receive, because you ask with wrong motives, that you may spend what you get on your pleasures" (James 4:3 NIV).

D. L. Moody touched on this when he explained, "Prayer does not mean that I am to bring God down to my thoughts and my purposes, and bend his government according to my foolish, silly, and sometimes sinful notions. Prayer means that I am. . .to enter into his counsel and carry out his purpose fully."

However, you may sincerely believe that your motives are good and wonder why God doesn't give you what you asked for. If you're living righteously, you might claim the verse, "No good thing will He withhold from those who walk uprightly" (Psalm 84:11 NKJV). But you may have no way of knowing what kind of changes might come about in your life if your prayer *was* answered. Jerry Sittser wrote in *When God Doesn't Answer Your Prayer* (2003), "Strange as it may sound, we need unanswered prayer. It is God's gift to us because it protects us from ourselves."

62. Will God still answer my prayers if I'm disobeying Him?

A leading reason God doesn't answer prayer is because there's sin in our lives. We're disobeying His will in some area. A verse in the last question reads, "No good thing will He withhold from those who walk uprightly" (Psalm 84:11 NKJV). Each coin has its flip side, and the reverse of this is: "Your iniquities have turned these things away, and your sins have withheld good from you" (Jeremiah 5:25 NKJV).

King David wrote, "If I had not confessed the sin in my heart, the Lord would not have listened" (Psalm 66:18 NLT). Unconfessed sins create a disconnect between us and God. If our relationship is damaged, He won't listen—at least not with intent to answer. Greg Laurie tells us in *Wrestling with God* (2003), "No matter how intense or fervent or long your prayers may be, if you have unconfessed sin in your life, your prayers are really going nowhere."

Here's another scripture that brings out this principle: "Surely the arm of the LORD is not too short to save, nor his ear too dull to hear. But your iniquities have separated you from your God; your sins have hidden his face from you, so that he will not hear" (Isaiah 59:1–2 NIV).

When God doesn't answer prayer, is it *always* because of sin in your life? Well, it's often the case—but not always. There are other reasons God doesn't answer prayer immediately.

If you're not aware of any sin, ask God to reveal to you if you're doing anything that's displeasing Him. Pray, "Search me, O God, and know my heart: try me, and know my thoughts: and see if there be any wicked way in me" (Psalm 139:23–24 KJV). Then confess any sin He reveals to you and repent of it.

63. Do I need to be perfect or holy before God will answer my prayers?

If that was the case, we'd all be sunk. None of our prayers would be answered. God says, "Be ye holy; for I am holy" (1 Peter 1:16 KJV), but being transformed into His image is an ongoing process. None of us will ever achieve perfection in this life. We all have sins and flaws that we're unaware of—or only vaguely aware of. And until we see them clearly, it's difficult to repent of them. But once we're aware of them, God's Holy Spirit convicts us to repent, and until we respond, they remain an issue between us.

Now, some of us are involved in a protracted battle against certain besetting sins that we're painfully aware of, but which we haven't yet fully overcome, much as we wish we had. These are often selfishness, covetousness, lust, apathy, a critical attitude, addictions, or disbelief. And, when we come before God in prayer, our hearts—not God, but *our own hearts*—condemn us that we're unworthy. Here's where the following principles apply:

"If our heart condemns us, God is greater than our heart, and knows all things. Beloved, if our heart does not condemn us, we have confidence toward God" (1 John 3:20–21 NKJV). Even if our conscience condemns us, God has promised to never leave us nor forsake us. That's never the issue. But our guilt *will* rob us of "confidence toward God" when we pray.

The good news is, however, if we persevere and begin to gain victories over our besetting sins, then our hearts no longer condemn us, and we *do* have confidence that our prayers will be answered. We then have faith to claim the very next verse: "And whatever we ask we receive from Him, because we keep His commandments and do those things that are pleasing in His sight" (1 John 3:22 NKJV).

64. Will God answer my prayers if I vow to change my ways?

This is commonly called "trying to make a deal with God." The connotation is that we're trying to barter with Him. We're desperate enough that we're willing to surrender a bad habit— or a disobedient lifestyle—on the condition that He comes through for us and answers our prayer.

Say, for example, we learn that a loved one has cancer. Or we're facing financial ruin. This shocks us so much that we resolve to pray every day, read our Bible faithfully, clean up our life, and attend church again. These are all things we need to do, and it often *does* take a crisis to cause us to rededicate our lives. But our motives are very important. If we're simply attempting to barter with God, then we may think that He "owes us." And if He *doesn't* answer our prayer, we can become bitter or very discouraged in our faith.

If we want to clean up our lives, we must allow God's Spirit free rein to do a genuine transformation. We must pray for Him to actually *change* us. We can't attempt to go bring about a "righteous lifestyle" in our own willpower, just for the sake of hoped-for miracles. If we've been living our lives far from God and disobedient to His Word, the first kind of prayer we should be praying is not for whatever miracle we desire, but for Jesus to take first place in our lives. (See question 18: "How will prayer affect me?")

Then, when we have reestablished our relationship with God, we stand a much greater chance that He will perform the miracle that we need.

65. Is lack of tithing why God doesn't answer my prayers and bless me?

In Old Testament times God commanded the Israelites to give 10 percent of their earnings to Him. "You must set aside a tithe of your crops—one-tenth of all the crops you harvest" (Deuteronomy 14:22 NLT). God promised to *bless* the Israelites if they tithed, but warned that they'd be under a *curse* if they failed to (Malachi 3:8–11). Not tithing simply wasn't an option.

Many churches believe that we today are still obligated to tithe. Although they agree that we're no longer under the Law but under grace (Romans 6:14), they teach that *this* particular law remains in effect. The New Testament is largely silent on the subject, but Jesus did say that the Pharisees were correct to tithe (Matthew 23:23). Now, if the law regarding tithing is still in effect, then yes, many financial problems are caused by a failure to tithe.

Other churches point out that the old Law is no longer in force (Galatians 3:24–25) and that nowhere in the New Testament are

Christians instructed to tithe. Instead, we're repeatedly told to give as much as we're able (2 Corinthians 8:12). Jesus talked a great deal about giving generously (Luke 6:38). Paul's instructions to Christians about giving, however, say nothing about giving 10 percent. He wrote: "You must each decide in your heart how much to give. And don't give reluctantly or in response to pressure. . . . And God will generously provide all you need. Then you will always have everything you need and plenty left over to share with others" (2 Corinthians 9:7–8 NLT). There are obviously *still* promises of financial blessing attached to our giving.

Whether you believe in tithing or not, part of being a Christian is giving to God and others—and God often *does* bless accordingly (2 Corinthians 9:6).

66. Do I need to forgive others before God will answer my prayers?

D. L. Moody said, "I firmly believe a great many prayers are not answered because we are not willing to forgive someone." Why did he believe this? Well, Jesus said: "And whenever you stand praying, if you have anything against anyone, forgive him, that your Father in heaven may also forgive you your trespasses" (Mark 11:25 NKJV). He told us to pray, "And forgive us our debts, as we forgive our debtors" (Matthew 6:12 NKJV), and added, "So if you are presenting a sacrifice at the altar in the Temple and you suddenly remember that someone has something against you, leave your sacrifice there at the altar. Go and be reconciled to that person. Then come and offer your sacrifice to God" (Matthew 5:23–24 NLT).

The greatest commandment is to love God, and if we're not doing *this*, we can't expect Him to answer our prayers. First John 4:20 (NIV) points out, "Whoever claims to love God yet hates a brother or sister is a liar."

If we have a bitter attitude towards someone, it not only corrupts us, but has a corrupting effect on people around us. That's why the Bible tells us to look "diligently lest any man fail of the grace of God; lest any root of bitterness springing up trouble you, and thereby many be defiled" (Hebrews 12:15 KJV).

Jesus warned not to curse someone. If we

hate someone, hold a grudge against them, and refuse to forgive them, we're likely to curse them. But Jesus said to do the opposite—pray for them and bless them. "Love your enemies, bless them that curse you, do good to them that hate you, and pray for them which despitefully use you, and persecute you" (Matthew 5:44 KJV).

To be sure, this isn't an easy commandment. But if we obey it we'll have greater faith when we pray that God will hear our prayers and bless *us*.

67. Does the devil fight and prevent the answers to prayer?

We sometimes don't get answers to prayer because Satan fights God's will. The prophet Zechariah saw this in a vision: "Then he showed me Joshua the high priest standing before the Angel of the LORD, and Satan standing at his right hand to oppose him" (Zechariah 3:1 NKJV).

Daniel once prayed for three weeks. God had sent an angel with the answer, and when he finally arrived he told Daniel that his prayers had been heard from the first day, but that a demon prince had fought to prevent him from getting through (Daniel 10:1–5, 12–13). If Daniel had become discouraged and stopped praying, the answer wouldn't have arrived.

However, faith-filled prayers are a force to be reckoned with, and the devil has learned that the most *effective* strategy is to discourage us from praying in the first place. As Samuel Chadwick said, "The one concern of the devil is to keep Christians from praying." George Müller added, "It is a common temptation of Satan to make us give up the reading of the Word and prayer when our enjoyment is gone; as if it were of no use to read the scriptures when we do not enjoy them, and as if it were no use to pray when we have no spirit of prayer."

But if he can't stop us from praying, then yes, he *will* most certainly fight us. Mary Warburton Booth explained: "Depend upon it, if you are bent on prayer, the devil will not leave you alone. He will. . .block you, and will surely find some hindrances, big or little or both. And we sometimes fail because we are ignorant of his devices. . . . I do not think he minds our praying about things if we leave it at that. What he minds, and opposes steadily, is the prayer that prays on until it is prayed through, assured of the answer."

68. How can I trust God for big miracles if He won't answer my small prayers?

Say you're praying for a loved one who has a serious illness. You pray every day, and because you understand that things of this magnitude take time, you don't expect a total change at once. But you trust steadfastly that your prayers *are* having an effect. Then you pray for a headache. If you aren't healed immediately you may take an aspirin—but then you might wonder, "How can I trust God for *big*, difficult miracles when He doesn't even answer my *small* prayers?"

Often we misjudge what requires only a brief prayer. How *long* would we be willing to pray for a headache to go away? Most of us wouldn't pray more than a minute. Apart from the time involved, it's hard for many of us to choose a miraculous solution when a natural remedy is readily available.

Dutch Sheets describes a time when his wife had a nonmalignant cyst, and their doctor wanted to operate. Dutch requested that he be given a chance to try prayer first. He prayed for *thirty* hours—and the cyst vanished! Would you have spent that long praying for something that could've been taken care of in a relatively simple operation? Dutch noted, "Some would believe that to be an unreasonable amount of time to pray for something—an hour a day for a month. . . . I'm only telling you what worked for me" (*Intercessory Prayer*, 1996).

Besides, God *does* answer many of our small prayers daily, but we often take the answers for granted and barely remember to thank Him. Sometimes we even forget that we prayed. That's why the Bible says, "Bless the Lord, O my soul, and forget not all his benefits" (Psalm 103:2 KJV). It's the prayers that aren't answered that often stand out and discourage us. So "forget not all God's benefits" and be encouraged by the prayers He *has* answered.

PERSISTING IN PRAYER

69. Why does God sometimes take so long to answer prayers?

One reason it takes time for God to answer prayer is because things must happen at a certain time—and if we learn patience and persevering faith in the process, these are definite benefits. The centurion Cornelius "prayed to God always," but his prayers only came up "for a memorial before God" at a specified time (Acts 10:1–4 NKJV). Also, when the saints cried out to God, asking how long before He answered their prayer, they were told to "rest a little while longer" (Revelation 6:11 NKJV).

Another reason God seems not to be answering our prayers, or takes so long to resolve a difficult situation, is because He's using the circumstances to work out a plan that we couldn't have even imagined.

One time, the ship Paul was sailing on was

caught in a terrific tempest and they were in utter darkness "for many days" and "all hope that [they] would be saved was finally given up" (Acts 27:20 NKJV). You can be certain that Paul was praying desperately. He was also afraid. Finally an angel appeared and told him *not* to be afraid, that he and all the other 275 passengers would survive. Paul then confidently declared, "I believe God that it will be just as it was told me" (verse 25). The Bible doesn't tell us how many more days they endured the storm, but finally on the fourteenth night (verse 27) they made it to land.

Why did God allow the storm to drive them so mercilessly, so long, and so far? Because it was His will that Paul evangelize the island of Malta—something that wouldn't have occurred had they sailed calmly to Rome (Acts 28:1, 7–10).

Adoniram Judson, the famous missionary to Burma, stated, "I never prayed sincerely and earnestly for anything but it came at some time; no matter at how distant a day, somehow, in some shape, probably the least I would have devised, it came."

70. Why do I often have to pray so persistently for things?

Why do you often have to pray and pray and pray for healing or a financial breakthrough or personal situations? Well, as you have most likely observed, sometimes God answers with a large, instantaneous miracle, and everything is resolved at once; most of the time, however, change comes gradually, in small increments.

Jesus told His disciples, "If you have faith as a mustard seed, you will say to this mountain, 'Move from here to there,' and it will move; and nothing will be impossible for you" (Matthew 17:20 NKJV; see also Luke 17:6). You might assume this verse is saying that if you have faith, you only need to pray *once* for an entire mountain to move, and it will instantly move. But if you've ever tried to move a mountain, you know that it usually doesn't happen that way.

Consider the Christians who faithfully prayed that the Iron Curtain would fall so that the Gospel could be preached freely in Communist nations. God eventually did the miracle—and that was a huge mountain moved!—but it took *decades* of prayer before it happened.

The key to understanding how faith like a tiny mustard seed can move mountains is found in a related parable. "Jesus said, 'How can I describe the Kingdom of God? . . . It is like a mustard seed planted in the ground. It is the smallest of all seeds, but it becomes the largest of all garden plants" (Mark 4:30–32 NLT).

Just as a mustard seed grows from a tiny speck into a gigantic herb, so faith has astonishing power and potential. But it usually takes *time*. It takes time and repeated doses of rain and sunshine, day after day, to cause a mustard seed to become a huge, tree-sized plant. Just so, it often takes time and repeated prayers for "mustard seed faith" to move mountain-sized obstacles.

This is why we have to persistently pray for certain things, day after day, even year after year.

71. What should I do when the answer to my prayer is delayed?

This is a very common human experience, and great men and women of God down through history have experienced having to wait months or years for their prayers to be answered. Let's look at what a number of them had to say on this subject.

D. L. Moody wrote in *Prevailing Prayer: What Hinders It?* (1884), "If we knock, God has promised to open the door and grant our request. It may be years before the answer comes; He may keep us knocking; but He has promised that the answer will come." The verse that Moody refers to is where Jesus promised, "Ask and it will be given to you; seek and you will find; knock and the door will be opened to you" (Matthew 7:7 NIV).

George Müller stated, "It is not enough to begin to pray, nor to pray aright; nor is it enough to continue for a time to pray; but we must patiently, believingly, continue in prayer until we obtain an answer."

Mary Slessor confessed, "I know what it is to pray long years and never get the answer—I had to pray for my father. But I know my heavenly Father so well I can leave it with Him for the lower fatherhood."

E. M. Bounds put it bluntly, saying, "He prays not at all, who does not press his plea."

C. H. Spurgeon said, "Continue in prayer, and though the blessing tarry, it must come; in God's own time it must appear to you."

Finally, Paul tells us in the Bible: "Pray in the Spirit at all times and on every occasion. Stay alert and be persistent in your prayers" (Ephesians 6:18 NLT). We must continue to pray and not give up on praying if we wish to see an answer to our prayers. (See also Luke 11:5–8; 18:1–7.)

72. Does it sometimes help to fast when we pray?

When facing serious situations, God's people frequently fasted. David fasted when he prayed for sick friends (Psalm 35:13), and Ezra and the Jews fasted when praying for protection for a dangerous journey (Ezra 8:21). Jesus Himself fasted and prayed forty days and forty nights (Matthew 4:2). Yet many people wonder whether modern Christians should fast.

Yes, Jesus expected us to and gave instructions on how to go about it: "But when you fast, put oil on your head and wash your face, so that it will not be obvious to others that you are fasting, but only to your Father" (Matthew 6:17–18 NIV). Paul advised married couples to temporarily abstain from intimate relations so "that you may give yourselves to fasting and prayer" (1 Corinthians 7:5 NKJV).

God will bless you for denying yourself, but it's not that refraining from food makes you more holy. However, it demonstrates a clear resolution to seek God without distractions— and allows you to give yourself wholeheartedly to prayer. Sometimes we need to pray harder for a breakthrough, and fasting facilitates that. Once, after casting out a demon, Jesus said, "This kind can come out by nothing but prayer and fasting" (Mark 9:29 NKJV).

Fasting is also helpful when seeking God's direction and when dedicating people to Him. The elders of the church at Antioch fasted and prayed for God's direction, and He spoke, telling them to send Barnabas and Paul out as missionaries (Acts 13:2–3). And Paul and Barnabas, when they "had appointed elders in every church, and prayed with fasting, they commended them to the Lord" (Acts 14:23 NKJV).

You don't need to totally abstain from food. Often you must keep working and can't be walking around lightheaded. Fasting can mean only eating necessary food. Daniel once fasted, eating "no rich food" or "meat or wine" for three weeks (Daniel 10:2–3 NLT).

73. What does it mean to "get desperate with God"?

Sometimes God doesn't answer prayer because we don't pray wholeheartedly. He promises, "And you will seek Me and find Me, when you search for Me with all your heart" (Jeremiah 29:13 NKJV). We're told to seek the Lord with all our heart, but if we *don't* pray wholeheartedly when we need to, God doesn't answer. Whereas if we *do* pray fervently He responds powerfully. "The earnest prayer of a righteous person has great power and produces wonderful results" (James 5:16 NLT).

David stated, "In my distress I called upon the LORD, and cried out to my God" (2 Samuel 22:7 NKJV), and some people wonder if this means literal crying. Does crying out with a whole heart mean emotions and tears? Often it does, but not always. The word "cried" here means to raise our voice, to call out urgently, not to weep. Nevertheless, we usually only pray that loud when moved by strong emotion.

When Christians talk about "getting desperate with God," they mean to be fully aware of how desperate a situation or a need is, and to turn to God and implore Him to rescue them. Often, as with many things in life, we procrastinate and let things slide, hoping they'll get better by themselves. But we can't be apathetic or indifferent in desperate situations.

Unfortunately, many people aren't in the habit of spending time in prayer. About the only times they actually *do* pray is when they find themselves in a crisis. Then they turn to God. But if your car broke down on a dark, lonely road, who would you feel more confident would come promptly to your aid—an acquaintance whom you haven't talked to in years, or a loving father whom you speak with daily?

74. What does it mean to "wrestle with God" in prayer?

The Bible says: "Then Jacob was left alone; and a Man wrestled with him until the breaking of day. Now when He saw that He did not prevail against him, He touched the socket of his hip; and the socket of Jacob's hip was out of joint as He wrestled with him." [With his hip painfully out of joint, Jacob could no longer wrestle, so simply locked his arms around the Man and refused to let go.] Jacob said, "I will not let You go unless You bless me!" (Genesis 32:24–26 NKJV).

Many Christians talk about "wrestling with God" until He gives us what we desire. But Dutch Sheets explains in his book, *Intercessory Prayer* (1996), "Scripture does not present this wrestling match as an example of how we are to. . .petition our heavenly Father. We are to approach Him with bold confidence (see Heb. 4:16), knowing He is our Friend and Father. We are to ask 'according to His will' (1 John 5:14), not try to wrestle from Him something He might not want to give."

We are to be like Jacob only in the sense that God *already* promises in His Word to bless us, so we refuse to let go of Him or His promise. Yes, we are to "take hold of" God. Isaiah once lamented that "there is no one who calls on Your name, who stirs himself up to take hold of You" (Isaiah 64:7 NKJV). The Bible also says, "You who call on the Lord, give yourselves no rest, and give him no rest till he establishes Jerusalem" (Isaiah 62:6–7 NIV).

We don't struggle against God, but strive to overcome our own lethargy and apathy. Paul said, "Now I beg you, brethren. . .that you strive together with me in prayers to God for me" (Romans 15:30 NKJV). If we wrestle *against* anyone, it's against evil spirits, the powers of darkness who try to prevent us from receiving God's blessing (Ephesians 6:12).

75. Is there a point where we've prayed enough and should stop?

You should stop asking God for something when you know that He's definitely sent the answer. When you know that God has answered your prayers, that's when it's time to stop *asking* Him and to start *thanking* Him.

(See question 34.) Whether you find that deep sense of assurance and full faith the *first* time you pray, or whether you receive it after prolonged seasons of prayer, it works out the same.

Mind you, you need to pray in faith each time you pray, since Jesus said, "Whatever you ask for in prayer, *believe* that you *have* received it, and it *will* be yours" (Mark 11:24 NIV, emphasis added). So yes, you need to believe each time you pray. But we're talking here about knowing when you've petitioned God about something enough and should stop praying.

Some people with great faith believe in only asking God for something *once*. Every time afterward when they come before Him, it's not to repeat their prayer, but simply to thank their heavenly Father for already hearing and answering. Even though they haven't seen the answer yet, they count is as done.

You might think, "I need to pray for things quite a bit before I have that level of confidence." Nevertheless, it can be faith building to focus on thanking God for a multitude of answered prayers, rather than always be petitioning Him. Thank Him for answered prayers of the past, thank Him for His promises to supply what you still need, and thank Him that, in His time, He *will* answer your present prayer. Believe it.

At some point in your prayers, you'll receive the full assurance that it's time to consider your request granted. It may be a conviction that grows slowly, or may be a sudden revelation, but you'll know when the time has come. Faith is knowing. And when you truly know something, you *know* that you know it.

BONUS QUESTION

Has this book helped your prayer life?

I trust that this book has helped you realize the need for prayer, and to understand that its power stems from a relationship with God, our Father, and His Son, Jesus. As you have seen, we don't receive things because of faith alone. Prayer is inseparably intertwined with several issues vital to the Christian life—faith, love, trust, perseverance, and obedience. All of these are essential to getting prayers answered.

It's God's will for us to have a deeper, richer life in Him. It's His will to supply our material needs as well as our spiritual needs—and He desires to use us to bless others. His Holy Spirit, dwelling in us, seeks to inspire us to pray for all these things.

And God answers prayer! As the veteran missionary Mary Slessor said, "My life is one

long daily, hourly, record of answered prayer."
But we must do our part. We must respond to
the Holy Spirit and stir ourselves up to pray
as needs arise. "You do not have because you
do not ask God" (James 4:2 NIV). D. L. Moody,
when looking forward to heaven, said, "Next
to the wonder of seeing my Savior will be, I
think, the wonder that I made so little use of
the power of prayer."

You may have been discouraged in the
past by experiences where prayers weren't
answered, but I trust that this book has
inspired your faith in God to begin praying
again, to know that you have the authority in
Christ to make such requests, and to persevere
until the answers come.